JIMMY CARTER

WE CAN HAVE PEACE IN THE HOLY LAND

—— •◆• ——

A Plan That Will Work

First published in Great Britain in 2010 by Simon & Schuster UK Ltd
A CBS COMPANY

1 3 5 7 9 10 8 6 4 2

Simon & Schuster UK Ltd
1st Floor
222 Gray's Inn Road
London
WC1X 8HB

www.simonandschuster.co.uk

Simon & Schuster Australia
Sydney

ISBN: 978-1-84983-064-5

Designed by Jaime Putorti
Printed by CPI Cox & Wyman, Reading, Berkshire RG1 8EX

To people of faith who still trust that God, with our help,
will bring peace to the Holy Land

———•◆•———

CONTENTS

———•◆•———

LIST OF MAPS

———•◆•———

xi

The blood of Abraham, God's father of the chosen, still flows in the veins of Arab, Jew, and Christian, and too much of it has been spilled in grasping for the inheritance of the revered patriarch in the Middle East. The spilled blood in the Holy Land still cries out to God—an anguished cry for peace.

—The Blood of Abraham, by Jimmy Carter

You cannot like the word, but what is happening is an occupation—to hold 3.5 million Palestinians under occupation. I believe that is a terrible thing for Israel and for the Palestinians. . . . It can't continue endlessly.

—Prime Minister Ariel Sharon, May 2003

There should be an end of the occupation that began in 1967. The agreement must establish Palestine as a homeland for the Palestinian people, just as Israel is a homeland for the Jewish people. These negotiations must ensure that Israel has secure, recognized and defensible borders. And they must ensure that the state of Palestine is viable, contiguous, sovereign, and independent. . . . Swiss cheese isn't going to work when it comes to the outline of a state.

—President George W. Bush, January 2008

We have to reach an agreement with the Palestinians, the meaning of which is that in practice we will withdraw from almost all the territories, if not all the territories. We will leave a percentage of these territories in our hands, but will have to give the Palestinians a similar percentage, because without that there will be no peace.

—Prime Minister Ehud Olmert, September 2008

STORM OVER A BOOK

I am writing another book about the Middle East because the new president of the United States is facing a major opportunity—and responsibility—to lead in ending conflict between Israel and its neighbors. The time is now. Peace is possible.

The normal path to resolving conflicts in this regional tinderbox should be through political leaders in Israel, Palestine, Syria, and Lebanon, with assistance when needed from Egypt, other Arab nations, and the international community. Yet for the past fifty years the United States has been widely recognized as the essential interlocutor that can provide guidance, encouragement, and support to those who want to find common ground. Unfortunately, most leaders in Washington have not been effective in helping the parties find peace, while making it harder for other potential mediators in Europe, the Near East, and the United Nations to intercede.

This peace effort should not be seen as a hopeless case. Five Nobel Peace Prizes have been won by leaders who negotiated successfully in 1979 and in 1993—one Egyptian, three Israelis, and one Palestinian. But the unpleasant fact is that there has been no tangible progress during the past decade and a half, despite significant efforts during the last years of the administrations of Bill Clinton and George W. Bush. Recent highly publicized peace talks between Israeli and Palestinian leaders have broached difficult issues but ultimately failed to narrow differences. At the same time, Israel and Syria became engaged early in 2007 in "indirect" conversations sponsored by Turkey, a fragile Gaza cease-fire has been implemented, and there has been an exchange of prisoners and the remains of others between Israel and Hezbollah but no further plans for easing tension between Israel and Lebanon.

As will be explained in the text, one of the notable developments in the region has been the repeated proposal by all twenty-two Arab nations to have normal diplomatic and commercial relations with Israel, provided major U.N. resolutions are honored. They have also said that modifications concerning controversial key issues could be considered in good-faith negotiations. This peace offer has been accepted by all Islamic nations and lauded by top U.S. officials, and Israelis have said it is a good basis for discussion.

If pursued aggressively with the full support of the United

States and other members of the International Quartet,* this Arab proposal could provide a promising avenue toward breaking the existing deadlock in promoting peace. This might make possible the formation of a multinational peace force in the West Bank to guarantee Israel's security, the release of prisoners (including a prominent jailed leader, Marwan Barghouti, who might heal divisions), updating the Palestine Liberation Organization (PLO) to include members from Hamas and other factions, and reconciliation between the two major Palestinian political parties. If a general framework could be forged, it would be difficult for minor factions to block a peace agreement.

Absent any real progress, conditions continue to fester, with Palestinians divided into two major parties. One group, Fatah, is "governing" in some parts of the West Bank not controlled by Israel (see Map 1, which shows actual control), supported officially by the international community as the dominant element of the PLO. Mahmoud Abbas was elected president of the Palestinian Authority to succeed Yasir Arafat, and he heads an interim government with most members from his Fatah Party. The other major group, Hamas, controls the small area of Gaza under the leadership of a group of local militants and more influential leaders of the politburo in Da-

---

* The United Nations, the United States, Russia, and the European Union.

mascus, Syria. There are loyal supporters of these two major parties in both Gaza and the West Bank, and some tentative efforts are detectable among them and from other Arab leaders to reunite the two factions. As will be explained in Chapter 10, unified Palestinians, with a workable government and a competent security force, are a prerequisite to any substantive peace agreement with Israel, but these initiatives have been blocked or undermined by mutual animosity and by opposition from Jerusalem and Washington.

It has not been possible for the weak and divided Palestinian leadership to eliminate acts of violence against Israel from within the occupied territories, and many Israelis are fearful for their personal safety and for the ultimate security of their nation. To defend themselves, they accept their government's policy of harsh reprisals and the constant expansion of settlements, although the majority of Israelis do not support the settlements as an alternative to peace. Except for some infrequent public statements and assurances given to me based on the prospect of an Israeli-PLO peace agreement, Hamas has not acknowledged Israel's right to exist and will not forgo violence as a means of ending the occupation of Palestinian territory.

For more than three decades, a major focus of my personal interests and political activities has been to help end the conflict among Israelis and their neighbors. As president of the United States and a leader of The Carter Center, I have had a special opportunity to study the complex and interrelated issues and to consult with leaders of all significant factions in the region who have been involved in these issues and will have to play key roles in reaching this elusive goal. I have learned some useful lessons, which I hope will help the reader understand the current situation more clearly.

Despite the recent lack of progress, I see this as a unique time for hope, not despair. The outlines of a peace agreement are clear and have broad international support. There is a remarkable compatibility among pertinent United Nations resolutions, previous peace agreements reached at Camp David and in Oslo, the publicly declared policy of the United States, the Geneva Accord, key goals of the International Quartet's Roadmap for Peace, and tentative proposals made by all Arab nations for reconciliation with Israel. Perhaps most important, there is an overwhelming common desire for peaceful and prosperous lives among the citizens of Israel, Palestine,* Lebanon, Syria, Jordan, and Egypt. Tentative steps are being taken or contemplated by these players, all waiting to be consummated with American leadership.

---

* I will sometimes use "the Holy Land" to mean the entire area between the Jordan River and the Mediterranean Sea, bounded on the north by Lebanon and on the south by Egypt. "Palestine" refers to the West Bank plus Gaza as defined by international agreements.

We already have a firm promise from our new president that he will make a personal effort for Middle East peace from the beginning of his administration. The United States will find all parties to the conflict—and leaders of other nations— eager to support strong, fair, and persistent leadership from Washington. This will not be easy. Everyone who engages in Middle East peacemaking is bound to make mistakes and suffer frustrations. Everyone must overcome the presence of hatred and fanaticism, and the memories of horrible tragedies. Everyone must face painful choices and failures in negotiations. Nevertheless, I am convinced that the time is ripe for peace in the region.

In the following pages I will describe—as succinctly and clearly as possible—the past history, my own personal involvement and observations, present circumstances, key players, and steps that can and must be taken by the president of the United States to realize this dream of peace, with justice, in the Holy Land. Experiences of the recent past offer valuable lessons as to what to avoid and how to proceed.

In fact, I learned a lot from the reaction to the publication of my book *Palestine Peace Not Apartheid*. When I completed the text of this book about Palestine in the summer of 2006, there had not been a day of peace talks for more than five years. In addition, there was no discussion in our country of the basic issues involved, and little interest in the subject. I and others representing The Carter Center had monitored three elections in the occupied territories and had gained an intimate knowledge of the people in the West Bank and Gaza and the issues that shaped their lives. I wanted a good forum to present my views, and I felt that explaining my book throughout the country would best meet this need.

I knew from experience how very difficult it was to sustain any objective political analysis in the United States of this important subject, primarily because few prominent political candidates or officeholders would voice any criticism of the current policies of the Israeli government. This meant that news media that were inclined to be objective had little to report other than occasional stories originated by their correspondents in the Middle East. On my visits to the region I found these reporters very knowledgeable, and they shared many of my concerns. I felt a personal responsibility to describe the situation, as best I could, to the American public, the news media, and members of Congress. I wanted to stimulate debate and perhaps some interest in reviving the moribund peace process. These were the underlying purposes of my book.

For most American readers, my book was the first time they had encountered both sides of these complex issues, including some rare criticism of Israeli policies in the occupied territories. Only by explaining both perspectives would it be possible to see how differences could be resolved and peace achieved.

As the text neared completion, I wanted a title that would be both descriptive and provocative. The working name on my computer was simply "Palestine Peace," but I didn't consider this to be adequate. I also tried "Land, Walls, Guns, or Peace," and finally decided on "Palestine Peace Not ——," and began to search for the most descriptive final word. Over a period of weeks it became clear that it was *apartheid*, a word that had been used many times by prominent Israelis, Israeli news media, and visiting observers. These included a former attorney general, scholars and legislators, editors of major newspapers, human rights organizations, and litigants who appealed to the Israeli Supreme Court. Many of them used and explained the word in harsher terms than I, pointing out that this occupation and oppression are contrary to the tenets of the Jewish faith and the basic principles of the nation of Israel. Nelson Mandela, Archbishop Desmond Tutu, and human rights activists from South Africa who visited the territories had used the same description.

I intended the word *apartheid* to describe a situation where two peoples dwelling on the same land are forcibly segregated from each other, and one group dominates the other. I thought the title and text would make it clear that the book was about conditions and events in the Palestinian territories and not in Israel and that the forced separation and domination of Arabs by Israelis were based on the acquisition of land and not on race, as had been the case in South Africa.

I realized that this might cause some concern in Israel and among Israel's supporters in America, but I intended to emphasize these distinctions in dozens of public presentations. Before this happened, I had copies delivered directly to the offices of all members of the U.S. Senate and House of Representatives. This proved to be a mistake. Without claiming to have read the text, some prominent Democrats condemned the title, and this provided the basis for many of the questions during my subsequent media discussions.

In more than a hundred interviews and many speeches, I found the questioning to be challenging and not unpleasant, but I was surprised and distressed when I was accused of being an anti-Semite, senile, a liar, a plagiarist, a racist, unfamiliar with the region, and a supporter of terrorism—these charges were made in public statements and in full-page newspaper advertisements. This was especially painful because some of the ad hominem attacks came from Jewish friends and organizations that had been supporters and allies while I was president and during the succeeding years.

In retrospect, I should have realized that the previous use of the word *apartheid* during the spirited debates in Israel had already aroused the sensitivity of many Israeli supporters in America about Israel's being equated with the racist regime in South Africa. To introduce it into an almost nonexistent discussion of the Palestinian issue in our country was highly controversial. Another factor was a carryover from my presidential years, of doubts about my commitment to Israel, as will be described in Chapters 2 and 3. Also, I underestimated the debating skills of those with whom I was now engaged, and was surprised by their personal attacks. Another mistake was not attempting to build earlier and broader political support among groups that were dedicated to peace in the Middle East.

I was eager to explain my thesis to every available audience, but I especially enjoyed the exchanges at a number of universities where I spoke and then answered questions from large groups of students. In each case I urged them and their professors to visit Palestine and ascertain whether I had exaggerated or mistakenly described the situation. Christian travel groups and other tourists were encouraged to visit Bethlehem and other holy sites within Palestine to observe the intrusive wall and the devastating impact of the occupation on the lives of Palestinian Christians.

Although I did not enjoy some of the criticisms, the book and my explanations of it did bring about a debate, which was my principal goal. In addition, President Bush finally announced a peace initiative, to begin with a conference in Annapolis, Maryland, with observers invited from a wide range of countries.

In August 2006, Jeff Skoll, chairman of Participant Productions, asked if I would permit a full-length documentary film to be made about my work at The Carter Center. He was the first president of eBay and more recently had produced the Al Gore film, *An Inconvenient Truth*, and several other motion pictures that accumulated eleven Oscar nominations that year. Later, I agreed to the proposal when he informed me that Jonathan Demme (*The Silence of the Lambs*, *Philadelphia*) had offered to direct the film.

Jonathan and I considered several theme options, including our Carter Center work in Africa and our Habitat for Humanity projects building homes in the area of the Gulf Coast damaged by Hurricane Katrina. He finally decided just to follow me around with high-definition cameras and record my daily activities. In November, his filming included the early days of travels to explain the Palestine book. There were dramatic news media interviews, discussions, arguments, speeches, book signings, and demonstrations that produced more than a hundred hours of recorded activities. These were interspersed with more tranquil scenes as I lectured at Emory University, interrelated with my neighbors and family, taught Bible lessons, made furniture, painted, exercised, and performed the duties of a farmer. Titled *Jimmy Carter Man from Plains*, the motion picture premiered in July 2007 and won several awards at film festivals. The high point of the film was my lecture and exchanges with the students at Brandeis University, which were charged with emotion and encapsulated the complex factors that must be addressed in the search for peace.

WE CAN HAVE PEACE IN THE HOLY LAND

Palestinian Land Restricted by Israeli Settlements and the Wall	
West Bank area west of the Wall (includes Israeli-occupied areas of East Jerusalem and the Latrun Valley)	**12%**
Settlement-controlled areas east of the Wall	**8%**
Jordan Valley settlement control	**26%**
Areas remaining for Palestinians	**54%**

Map 1

Israel's Wall and
Settlements
as of
July 2008

Mediterranean Sea

Netanya

ISRAELI OCCUPIED
WEST BANK

Rehan
Jenin
Mevo Dotan
Mehola

Tulkarm
Avne
Hefez
Elon
Moreh
Hamra

Kedumim
Nablus
Itamar
Massua

Qalquilya
Yizhar

Alfe Menashe
Elkana
Ariel
Ma'ale
Efrayim

Tel Aviv
Salfit
Eli

Bet Arieh
Shilo

ISRAEL

Nili
Talmon
Beit
El
Ofra

Modi'in
Illit
Ramallah

Givat
Ze'ev
Geva
Binyamin
Jericho

Jerusalem ★
Ma'ale
Adumim

Har Gilo
Betar
Bethlehem

Tekoa

Kfar
Etzion
Efrat

Karme
Zur
Asfar

Adora
Mitzpe
Shalem

Hebron
Kiryat Arba

Otni'el

Tene

JORDAN VALLEY

Jordan River

JORDAN

LATRUN VALLEY

Dead
Sea

—— Wall completed
∙∙∙∙∙ Wall under construction
—— Wall trajectory approved
by Israeli cabinet
1967 Boundary
(Green Line)
Under Israeli settlement
control
Israeli settlements

0   5   10 miles
0   5   10 kilometers

N
W   E
S

FROM ABRAHAM'S JOURNEYS TO THE SIX-DAY WAR

Current events in the Middle East can best be understood if we start with a brief review of the history of the region. Since I was a little child, I have been familiar with the journey of Abraham from Ur through Haran to Canaan about 2000 B.C., the Israelites' enslavement in Egypt about five hundred years later, the powerful rule of Kings David and Solomon about 1000 B.C., the later captivity of the Hebrews by the Babylonians, Assyrians, and Persians, and their return from exile to rebuild Jerusalem and the Temple about five hundred years before the birth of Jesus Christ. My father and others taught me every Sunday about the other great prophets who relayed God's word to his chosen people, mostly during the period of their exile, and who Christians believe were preparing for the coming of the Messiah, Jesus Christ, a descendant of David.

The Greeks conquered the region three centuries before the earthly ministry of Jesus, and the Jews established an independent Judea that existed until the Roman conquerors came about fifty years later. They ruled with a firm hand, insisting on the maintenance of peace and the proper payment of taxes. There was a Jewish revolt in A.D. 70, which was crushed by the Romans, who destroyed the Temple. After another revolt in A.D. 134, many Jews were forced into exile, and the Romans named its province Syria-Palaestina while the Jews preferred that it be called Eretz Israel.

A few churches were formed by early Christians from Jerusalem and struggled for survival around the Mediterranean coast to Rome. After Emperor Constantine was converted to Christianity, circa A.D. 325, the powerful leader imposed his religious beliefs throughout the kingdom. This Christian advantage in the region was largely overcome after the Prophet Muhammad (570–632) founded the Islamic faith and united the Arabian Peninsula, and his followers spread their political domination and religion throughout Syria-Palestine, Persia, Egypt, North Africa, and southern Europe. Christian crusaders launched massive military crusades to retake Jerusalem and established dominion over Palestine in 1099. However, Saladin, sultan of Egypt, retook the Holy City in 1187, and, after 1291, Muslims controlled Palestine until the end of World War I. Then the French and British played major roles in the Middle East and spread their influence as spoils of victory.

Great Britain issued the Balfour Declaration in 1917, promising a Jewish national home in Palestine, with respect for the rights of non-Jewish Palestinians. In 1922, the League of Nations confirmed a British Mandate over Iraq, Palestine, and Jordan, and a French Mandate over Syria and Lebanon. Transjordan became an autonomous kingdom. Later, Palestinian Arabs demanded a halt to Jewish immigration and a ban on land sales to Jews, and in 1939 Britain announced severe restrictions on the Zionist movement and land purchases in Palestine. Violence erupted from Jewish militants, some led by Menachem Begin, the future prime minister of Israel.

It is impossible to comprehend the enormity of the unspeakable crime against humanity—the Holocaust perpetrated by Adolf Hitler—but I studied the superb works of Elie Wiesel and other survivors early in my political career to learn as much as possible about it. More recently, in an intriguing book, *The Invisible Wall*, my secretary of treasury Michael Blumenthal described the experiences of Jews in Germany based on his own life and those of members of his family, beginning in 1640. Mike was born in Germany in 1926 and escaped the Nazis as a teenager by moving with his family and other Jews to a ghetto in Shanghai in 1939 after his father escaped from the Nazi prison at Buchenwald. Eight years later the Blumenthals were able to come to the United States.

When Hitler became chancellor of the Third Reich, in 1933, Mike wrote:

> Germany's Jews had made an astonishing impact on Germany in many fields and far beyond the country's borders, but there had never been more than about 600,000 of them—a tiny minority of no more than one percent of the German people. During the first eight years after Hitler seized power, more than 300,000 managed to flee and some 70,000 died; since the Jewish population was over-aged, the rate of deaths greatly exceeded that of births. So, when the doors finally closed in 1941 and escape was no longer possible, there were only 163,000 Jews left. Most were deported to the East, and very few survived. Thousands took their own lives.

In 1947, Britain decided to let the United Nations determine what to do about Palestine, which was partitioned between Jews and Arabs, with Jerusalem and Bethlehem as international areas. By this time, Egypt, Syria, Lebanon, and Transjordan were independent states.

A year later the British Mandate over Palestine terminated and the State of Israel was proclaimed. The troops of all the surrounding countries—Egypt, Syria, Jordan, and Lebanon—attacked the tiny new nation that had no regular army, and were joined by Iraqis and other Arabs. Fighting for their lives and their nation, Israelis finally prevailed after a year of conflict, and a cease-fire was negotiated with expanded Israeli territory (about 77 percent of the total) accepted by the Arab adversaries. The armistice line became known as the "Green Line," accepted by Israel and confirmed as legal by the international community. Jordan annexed East Jerusalem and the area between Israel and the Jordan River (about 22 percent), and Egypt assumed control over the Gaza Strip (about one percent).

The United Nations estimates that about 710,000 Arabs left voluntarily or were ejected from Israel, and troops then barred their return and razed more than five hundred of their ancestral villages. This became known by the Arabs as the *naqba*, or catastrophe, and U.N. General Assembly Resolution 194 established a conciliation commission and asserted that refugees wishing to return to their homes and live in peace should be allowed to do so, that compensation should be paid to others, and that free access to the holy places should be assured. The treatment of these refugees and their descendants has remained a major source of dispute.

In 1956, Egypt nationalized the Suez Canal, and Israel,

Britain, and France occupied the canal area. Pressure from the international community forced all foreign troops to withdraw from Egyptian territories by the next year, and U.N. forces were assigned to patrol strategic areas of the Sinai Peninsula.

The Palestine Liberation Organization (PLO) was established in 1964, committed to liberating the homeland of the Palestinian people.

In May 1967, Egypt expelled the U.N. monitoring force from the Sinai, moved a strong military force to the border, closed the Straits of Tiran to Israeli shipping, and signed a mutual defense treaty with Jordan and Syria. Israel responded by launching a preemptive attack that destroyed Egypt's air force. When Jordan and Syria joined in the combat, Israel gained control within six days of the Sinai, the Golan Heights, Gaza, and the West Bank including East Jerusalem.

Six months later, U.N. Security Council Resolution 242 was passed, confirming the inadmissibility of the acquisition of land by force and calling for Israel's withdrawal from occupied territories, the right of all states in the region to live in peace within secure and recognized borders, and a just solution to the refugee problem (see Appendix 1).

MY EARLY INVOLVEMENT
WITH ISRAEL

While I was governor of Georgia, in 1973, I traveled with my wife, Rosalynn, throughout Israel and the occupied territories as guests of Prime Minister Golda Meir and General Yitzhak Rabin, hero of the Six-Day War. We visited the usual tourist spots and Christian holy places but, more important, several kibbutzim, including a relatively new one on the escarpment of the Golan Heights. We enjoyed extensive discussions with these early Jewish settlers and learned that there were about fifteen hundred of them living on occupied Arab land at that time. The general presumption among Israeli leaders was that the settlers would withdraw as other provisions of U.N. Resolution 242 were honored. During the more official portion of our visit we rode torpedo boats at Haifa and participated in a graduation ceremony for young soldiers at Bethel, and I had

Map 2

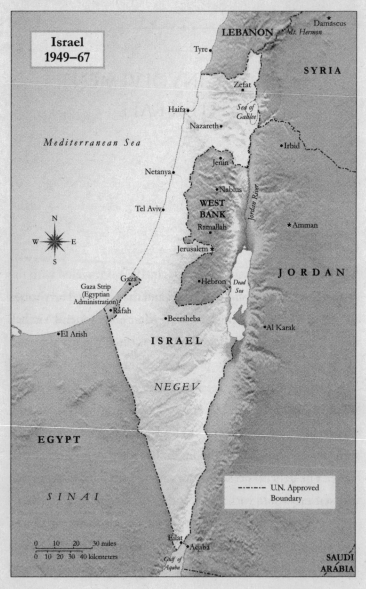

Israel
1949–67

Damascus
LEBANON · Mt. Hermon
Tyre
SYRIA
Zefat
Haifa
Sea of Galilee
Nazareth
Mediterranean Sea
Irbid
Jenin
Netanya
Nablus
WEST BANK
Tel Aviv
Ramallah
Amman
Jordan River
Jerusalem
JORDAN
Gaza Strip (Egyptian Administration)
Gaza
Hebron
Dead Sea
Rafah
Beersheba
Al Karak
El Arish
ISRAEL
NEGEV
EGYPT
SINAI
N W E S
U.N. Approved Boundary
0 10 20 30 miles
0 10 20 30 40 kilometers
Eilat
Aqaba
Gulf of Aqaba
SAUDI ARABIA

detailed "secret" briefings from Israeli intelligence chief General Chaim Bar-Lev, General Rabin, Prime Minister Meir, and one of the world's most eloquent diplomats, Abba Eban.

This visit to the Holy Land made a lasting impression on me. I had taught Bible lessons on Sundays since I was a midshipman at the U.S. Naval Academy, divided equally between Hebrew scriptures and the New Testament. Like almost all other American Christians, I believed that Jewish survivors of the Holocaust deserved their own nation and had the right to live peacefully with their neighbors. This homeland for the Jews was compatible with the teachings of the Bible. These beliefs gave me an unshakable commitment to the security and peaceful existence of Israel.

I was making plans to run for president during the year of our visit to Israel, and I began a detailed study of political developments in the region. The most significant event during 1973 was the apparent expulsion by Egypt of Soviet advisers, based on a public allegation by President Anwar Sadat that their benefactor refused to provide the advanced weapons needed for Egypt's defense. In fact, most Soviet military experts were simply redeployed to Syria, with the consent of the Egyptian government, while the two nations began to plan an attack on Israel.

In October 1973 (during the Yom Kippur holidays), Israeli forces were struck simultaneously in the Sinai and the Golan Heights, catching Prime Minister Golda Meir and her government by surprise. After sixteen days of intense combat, various disengagement agreements followed, negotiated mostly by U.S. secretary of state Henry Kissinger. U.N. Security Council Resolution 338 was passed, confirming Resolution 242 and calling for international peace talks, likely sponsored primarily by the United States and the Soviet Union. Although Arab military attacks were successfully repulsed, this ended the euphoria in Israel following its victory in the Six-Day War of 1967 and restored the pride and confidence of Egypt and Syria. General Rabin replaced Meir as Israel's prime minister while other events were shaping the situation I would inherit as president.

In 1974, the Arab summit at Rabat proclaimed the Palestine Liberation Organization (PLO) the sole legitimate representative of the Palestinian people, who were scattered throughout the region. This was soon followed by a public pledge from the U.S. government to have no contacts with leaders of the PLO until they adopted U.N. Resolution 242 and acknowledged Israel's right to exist in peace. When civil war erupted in Lebanon in 1975, the international community, including the United States, approved Syria's sending troops into the troubled country to establish order. In June 1976, our ambassador to Lebanon was kidnapped and murdered, his successor was forced to return to Washington, and American nationals had to be evacuated from the country by sea.

• • •

Except for our tour of the Holy Land when I was governor, I was not directly involved in affairs of the Middle East, but the region was of great interest to me and I probed for new ideas. At a 1975 meeting of the Trilateral Commission* in Japan, I made some impromptu comments advocating balanced and much more aggressive steps toward peace. Afterward, the commission's executive director, Zbigniew Brzezinski, came and offered to help me develop my ideas. A year later, during my campaign for president, he and Stu Eizenstat assisted me in preparing my basic speech about the Middle East, which I first delivered in an Orthodox synagogue in Elizabeth, New Jersey. (I remember that it was near a shipyard where some of our nation's submarines had been built.) Wearing a blue yarmulke, I said:

> The land of Israel has always meant a great deal to me. As a boy I read of the prophets and martyrs in the Bible—the same Bible that we all study together. As an American I have admired the State of Israel and how she, like the United States, opened her doors to the homeless and the oppressed. . . . All people of goodwill can agree it is

---

* A private group of leaders from Japan, North America, and Europe.

time—it is far past time—for permanent peace in the Middle East. . . . A real peace must be based on absolute assurance of Israel's survival and security. As President, I would never yield on that point. The survival of Israel is not just a political issue, it is a moral imperative.

Although President Gerald Ford was known as a friend of Israel, neither he nor his predecessors had considered a strong move toward a comprehensive peace agreement. Instead of the gradualist approach being pursued by him and Secretary of State Kissinger, I argued during the general election campaign that "a limited settlement, as we have seen in the past, still leaves unresolved the underlying threat to Israel. A comprehensive settlement is needed—one that will end the conflict between Israel and its neighbors once and for all." In this same speech, I went on to say, "There is a humanitarian core within the complexities of the Palestinian problem. Too many human beings, denied a sense of hope for the future, are living in makeshift and crowded camps where demagogues and terrorists can feed on their despair."

I continued this theme with a number of audiences, but my more comprehensive approach, including Palestinian rights, received little attention from the news media. During the second of our three presidential debates, in October, I pushed hard on the Middle East issue, including the Arab boycott. One of Ford's strong supporters, Rita Hauser, commented two years later, "It was astounding to me that Carter made so much in that second debate of what I will call the Jewish issues. . . . I think it made a great difference because the Jews were very puzzled by Carter—to this day they remain puzzled by Carter—and he was not a man to whom there would be a natural attraction."

It was well known among my White House staff and cabinet officers even before inauguration day that peace in the Middle East would be at the top of my foreign affairs agenda for prompt action. Looking back on my presidency and the succeeding years, I believe the most important single mission in my political life has been to assist in bringing peace to Israel and its neighbors and to promote human rights. I didn't have an adequate comprehension in my earlier political days that an almost inevitable conflict would evolve between the two as I dealt with Israelis and Palestinians. Once in office, I lost no time in beginning this work.

The issue of Middle East peace was fairly dormant in January 1977, but many of my inherited duties were directly and adversely affected by events in the troubled region. There had been four major wars during the preceding twenty-five years led or supported by Egypt, the only Arab country (with Soviet military backing) that had the status of a formidable challenger. Also, Jews in the Soviet Union were singled out for persecution, and only in rare cases were they permitted to emigrate to Europe, the United States, or other free nations. There was a lack of any concerted effort by our government to bring peace to America's closest ally in the Middle East, and, in fact, there were no demands on me as a successful candidate to initiate such negotiations. Having visited the Holocaust museum Yad Vashem on my visit to Israel, I was aware that there had never been any memorial site in America as a reminder of the despicable events of the Nazi Holocaust.

An especially reprehensible situation that I faced was the embargo by Arab members of the Organization of the Petroleum Exporting Countries (OPEC), not only to constrain the distribution of oil to our country but to boycott American businesses that conducted trade with Israel. Amazingly, our government was acquiescent and many business leaders had signed agreements to comply with this obnoxious restraint. In my second debate with President Ford during our general election campaign, I had stated, "I believe that the boycott of American businesses by the Arab countries because those businesses trade with Israel is an absolute disgrace. This is the first time that I remember, in the history of our country, when we've let a foreign country circumvent or change our Bill of Rights. I'll do everything I can as President to stop the boycott. . . . It's not a matter of diplomacy or trade with me; it's a matter of morality." I also stated that if any country should ever again declare such an embargo against our citizens I would consider it "an economic declaration of war and would respond instantly and in kind. I would not ship that country anything. No weapons, no spare parts for weapons, no oil-drilling rigs, no oil pipe, no nothing."

I realized at the time that many European nations were complying with the Arab boycott, and I hoped that my position might evolve into a more intimate relationship between the United States and Israel. I worked closely and successfully on this issue with some key members of the House and Senate, the Anti-Defamation League, and other Jewish organizations. My biggest problem was with leaders of the Business Roundtable, some of whose members were fearful of losing their lucrative business with the more powerful Arab nations.

The most sensitive political issue I faced was what could be done about the plight of the Palestinians. It had seemed to me during my visit to the region four years earlier that there was a consensus within Israel that the basic principles of United Nations resolutions would be honored, including the withdrawal of Israel from occupied territories. It was obvious that this would leave the Palestinians with some kind of homeland, but it had not been defined. Jordan administered many affairs in the West Bank, but for most Arabs the Palestine

Liberation Organization represented the political interests of Palestinians. I was constrained by previous American commitments not to recognize the PLO by diplomatic contact or acknowledgment of its legitimacy, so my only alternative was to deal with the Palestinian people through Syria, Jordan, and Egypt as their surrogates. Neither the Israelis nor the Palestinians were willing to consider the peaceful existence of the others as a governmental entity.

I discussed all these complex issues with my political advisers, including my wife, Rosalynn, and with other leaders who were knowledgeable about the region and its history. Almost invariably, they advised me to stay out of the Middle East controversy, at least "until a second term." I was not naïve and realized that the subject could be an insoluble political quagmire, destined to require a substantial portion of my time with doubtful chances of success. Of more political importance was the potential negative reaction of the American Jewish community, an extremely valuable source of leadership and support within the Democratic Party. I rationalized my decision to proceed with the belief that even partial success would bring political benefits.

I was determined to make an effort to resolve the regional problem on a more immediate and comprehensive basis than had been attempted earlier. One major constraint on my initiatives as president was that the previous administration had spelled out the forum for peace talks: in Geneva, Switzerland, and in partnership with the Soviet Union. This deterrent was at least partially counterbalanced by my confidence in Prime Minister Rabin, whom I knew well and admired as a wise and courageous leader.

We had discussions with Soviet ambassador Anatoly Dobrynin and foreign minister Andrei Gromyko about our joint obligations in the Middle East, but my talks with them were somewhat strained because I also had begun to communicate publicly with noted Jewish human rights heroes like Andrei Sakharov and to confront Soviet leaders persistently on behalf of Natan Sharansky and others whom I considered to be prisoners of an oppressive regime. One of the most famous photographs of that era was of Sakharov holding my handwritten letter in front of the camera lens. This widely publicized campaign increased tension between me and Soviet president Leonid Brezhnev, but my persistence may have borne fruit. Within two years, annual Jewish immigration from Russia to the United States increased from a few hundred to more than fifty thousand. I was grateful when Sharansky was released from a Soviet labor camp and gave our policies credit for having saved his life.

I extended an early invitation to Prime Minister Yitzhak Rabin, whom I already knew well as my visitor and also host while I was governor, to come to Washington. I had bold plans and was eager to obtain his full support before I embarked on the effort. Here are my personal diary notes:

> Prime Minister Rabin came over from Israel. I've put in an awful lot of time studying the Middle East question and was hoping that Rabin would give me some outline of what Israel ultimately hopes to see achieved in a permanent peace agreement. I found him very timid, very stubborn, and also ill at ease. . . . When he went upstairs with me, just the two of us, I asked him to tell me what Israel wanted me to do when I met with the Arab leaders and if there was something specific, for instance, that I could propose to Sadat. He didn't unbend at all, nor did he respond. It seems to me that the Israelis, at least Rabin, don't trust our government or any of their neighbors. I guess there's some justification for this distrust. I've never met any of the Arab leaders, but am looking forward to seeing if they are more flexible than Rabin.—March 7, 1977

My discouragement was somewhat assuaged when it was reported in the news media that Rabin and his wife were being charged with having illegal bank accounts in America. I presumed that this was the cause of his discomfort and decided to proceed with some public proposals: two borders for Israel, the 1967 line and another in the West Bank with a safety zone in between; Israel's ultimate withdrawal to the 1967 borders but with small adjustments for security purposes; a termination of belligerence toward Israel by its Arab neighbors and a recognition of its right to exist in peace; and free trade, tourist travel, and cultural exchange among the nations in the Middle East.*

As had all my predecessors in the White House starting with Lyndon Johnson, I considered Israeli settlements in the occupied territories to be both illegal and an obstacle to peace.

On March 16, less than two months after taking office, I answered, extemporaneously, a question in a town meeting in Clinton, Massachusetts, about my plans for the Middle East. With very few changes, the same answer could be given today. Here is what I said:

> The first prerequisite of a lasting peace is the recognition of Israel by her neighbors, Israel's right to exist, and Israel's right to exist in peace. That means that over a period of months or years the

---

* It is interesting that these proposals have some similarity to the temporary Israeli barrier now being built within the West Bank and a key proposal in the Geneva Accord (see Chapter 5) that minor permanent adjustments be made to the pre-1967 border.

borders between Israel and Syria, Israel and Lebanon, Israel and Jordan, Israel and Egypt must be opened up to travel, to tourism, to cultural exchange, to trade, so that no matter who the leaders might be in those countries, the people themselves will have formed a mutual understanding and comprehension and a sense of a common purpose to avoid the repetitious wars and death that have afflicted the region so long. That's the first prerequisite of peace.

The second one is very important and very, very difficult, and that is the establishment of permanent borders for Israel. The Arab countries say that Israel must withdraw to the pre-1967 borderlines; Israel says that they must adjust those lines to some degree to insure their own security. That is a matter to be negotiated between the Arab countries on the one side and Israel on the other. But borders are still a matter of great trouble and a matter of great difficulty, and there are strong differences of opinion now.

And the third ultimate requirement for peace is to deal with the Palestinian problem. The Palestinians claim up until this moment that Israel has no right to be there, that the land belongs to the Palestinians, and they've never yet given up their publicly professed commitment to destroy Israel. That has to be overcome.

There has to be a homeland provided for the Palestinian refugees who have suffered for many, many years. And the exact way to solve the Palestinian problem is one that first of all addresses itself right now to the Arab countries and then, secondly, to the Arab countries negotiating with Israel.

These three major elements have got to be solved before a Middle Eastern solution can be prescribed.

I want to emphasize one more time, we offer our good offices. I think it's accurate to say that of all the nations in the world, we are the one that's most trusted, not completely, but most trusted by the Arab countries and also Israel. I guess both sides have some doubt about us. But we'll have to act kind of as a catalyst to bring about their ability to negotiate successfully with one another.

I also announced my plans to meet with leaders from Egypt, Jordan, Syria, and Saudi Arabia within the next two months. A few days later I went to New York to address the U.N. General Assembly and shook hands with the official representative of the PLO. This aroused some negative comments but did not violate the existing U.S. commitment not to recognize or negotiate with the PLO until it acknowledged Israel's right to exist and agreed to U.N. Resolution 242. I considered this resolution to be the foundation for any future agreement because it emphasized the inadmissibility of the acquisition of territory by war and called for a just and lasting peace in the area, withdrawal of Israel from territories occupied in the Six-Day War, guaranteed territorial inviolability and political independence of all states in the area, and a just settlement of the Palestinian refugee issue.

I was encouraged when King Hussein of Jordan visited me in April, and I recorded in my diary:

> At this time my basic plan is to meet with the leaders of the nations involved, completing this round in May, then put together our own concept of what should be done in the Middle East, let [Secretary of State] Cy Vance make a trip around the area to consult with leaders, listening more than he talks, and then put as much pressure as we can bring to bear on the different parties to accept the solution that we think is fair.—April 25, 1977

Next on my list was Syrian president Hafez al-Assad, who responded to my invitation by informing me that he never intended to visit America. I flew from a summit meeting in London to Geneva and spent almost four hours in an intense conversation with him. He was constructive with his ideas and surprisingly flexible concerning some of the sensitive issues I raised. I detected a negative and somewhat competitive attitude toward Egypt, and soon learned that as Sadat became more supportive, Assad would move in the opposite direction. It was obvious that he had very close ties with the Soviet Union, but at the time I did not consider this a negative factor. He was insistent that the PLO be represented at any future peace talks, an opinion that had been expressed strongly by Foreign Minister Gromyko.

In subsequent meetings with Crown Prince Fahd of Saudi Arabia, the prince assured me that I would get full support for any tangible moves toward peace but that the plight of the Palestinians was his major concern. It was clear that the Saudis would never be in the forefront of any bold moves, but at that time this did not seem necessary.

The most potent criticism at this time came from the American Jewish community and fervent supporters of Israel within the U.S. Congress. Although I had not departed in any substantive way from the policies of earlier presidents, my approach was much more vigorous and we were addressing some of the controversial issues, such as secure and recognized borders and a "homeland" for the Palestinians, with more un-equivocal language.* Jewish leaders were also concerned about my apparently friendly meetings with so many Arabs and the uncertainty of the future policies of Yitzhak Rabin. I met with many influential American Jews who were privately supportive and, like the Arab leaders, urged me to explore all avenues that might lead to peace. But in any public discussion of a controversial issue they would side with Israeli government policy and condemn me for being biased or just "even-handed" in our concern about both Palestinian rights and Israeli security.

I finally decided to appeal to Senator Hubert Humphrey, and he began to bring Senators Abraham Ribicoff, Jacob Javits, Clifford Case, and other dedicated supporters of Israel for private discussions with me in the White House as we developed specific ideas to be pursued during my meetings with Arab and Israeli leaders. These key senators and a few House members, including Stephen Solarz, gave me their full support—provided Israel's security and full recognition as a free nation were preserved.

---

* In those days there was no consideration by the Palestinians of an independent state alongside Israel.

3

PEACE AT CAMP DAVID

President Anwar Sadat visited me from Egypt a month after Rabin and brought a new and shining light to the issue of peace. We formed an almost immediate personal friendship that was to last a lifetime. In a private session upstairs in the White House after the formal state banquet, he and I explored possibilities previously forbidden—at least as a package—including demilitarized zones on Egyptian territory, an end to the Arab boycott against Israel, moderation in the PLO ranks, possible deviation from the 1967 borders, an undivided but shared Jerusalem, and direct peace talks between Egypt and Israel "provided the Palestinian issue is resolved." I pushed him hard on my ultimate goals: Israeli use of the Suez Canal, his diplomatic recognition of Israel, and exchange of ambassadors—and he finally agreed that these goals might be possible "after five years of peace." He pushed me on standing up to political pressures in the United States, and I told him I would face any necessary political risks to reach a peace settlement. Later, as we prepared for bed, I told Rosalynn that this had been my best day as president.

Immediately after this visit, Rabin announced that he would not seek reelection, and Likud leader Menachem Begin was elected as Israel's sixth prime minister. The American Jewish community and I were equally shocked to see an end to the pattern of leaders who had previously been so intimately known within our country. The new prime minister had been a radical firebrand, previously named by the British as one of the most notorious terrorists in the region after a bombing by his organization in 1946 killed almost a hundred people in the King David Hotel in Jerusalem. None of us knew what to expect. Sadat reported to me that he asked Eastern Europeans who knew Begin two questions: "Is he honest?" and "Is he a strong man?" He was reassured when both answers were "Yes."

In preparing for my meeting with Prime Minister Begin, I learned all I could about him and also studied a current public opinion poll in Israel. Sixty-three percent of the Israelis wanted peace with the Arabs, 52 percent thought that the Palestinians deserved a homeland, and 43 percent said the homeland ought to be on the West Bank of the Jordan River, while others preferred the East Bank (Jordan). By a 45–45 split, the people of Israel thought they should negotiate directly with the PLO if the PLO would recognize Israel's right to exist.

When I met with Begin in July, we had a pleasant and surprisingly productive session, and I wrote:

> I found him to be quite congenial, dedicated, sincere, deeply religious. . . . I think Begin is a very good man and, although it will be difficult for him to change his position, the public opinion polls that we have from Israel show that the people there are quite flexible and genuinely want peace.—July 19, 1977

I considered Begin to be interested in my peace plan, politically courageous, and remarkably blunt and incisive. I outlined my key proposals to him, including a truly comprehensive agreement encompassing all Israel's neighbors; compliance with U.N. Resolution 242; open borders and free trade; Israel's withdrawal from occupied territory to secure borders; and a Palestinian political entity to be created. My presumption was that Israel would have to withdraw its forces to the pre-1967 borders, and Begin did not reject this or my other proposals outright. However, he asked, pending more precise discussions, that I not make this same withdrawal assumption in my subsequent discussions with the Soviets or Arab leaders. He said he could possibly agree with all except the Palestinian entity.

I emphasized strongly that Israeli settlements were both illegal and the primary obstacle to peace; he did not respond. Unfortunately, the prime minister publicly recognized some of the West Bank settlements as permanent when he returned home. Israeli foreign minister Moshe Dayan came to see me in September and promised that no more civilians would go into the settlements, only people in uniform into the military sites. This was a major concession, but unfortunately it was not the position of the prime minister.

I continued to wrestle with the problem of a Geneva conference, approved by the United Nations, over which we and the Soviets were to preside. The Israelis were very fearful of Soviet bias toward Syria and the other Arabs, Sadat felt alienated from Moscow, and Syrian president Assad announced that he would attend only as part of an Arab delegation with the PLO on an equal footing with other Arabs—which the Israelis would never accept. I decided to appeal directly to Sadat to take a bold initiative. After we discussed and rejected the possibility of shifting the Geneva meeting to Cairo or East Jerusalem, Sadat announced that he was prepared to go to Jerusalem. Begin extended an invitation through me for the Egyptian president to speak directly to the Israeli Knesset, and Sadat did so in November.

The reaction to Sadat's relatively demanding rhetoric—

even emphasizing the maximum Arab demands for full Palestinian rights—was euphoria in Israel, Egypt, America, and the Western world but condemnation in the Arab nations. Syria broke off diplomatic relations with Egypt, while top officials in Syria, Libya, and Iraq called for Sadat's assassination. After a week or two it seemed that the only tangible result of his visit would be a death knell for the comprehensive peace talks in Geneva. We had a full-court press among Middle East leaders throughout December, and Sadat and Begin had a return meeting in Ismailia, Egypt. Begin seemed satisfied with the results, but Sadat considered the nonsubstantive session to be a complete failure and a setback for the peace process, since Begin insisted on keeping Israeli settlers in Egypt's Sinai.

Over the 1978–79 New Year holidays I made personal visits in the region to meet with King Hussein of Jordan, King Khalid of Saudi Arabia, and the Shah of Iran. They were strongly (and secretly) supportive of our continued efforts for peace. On the way home I stopped in Aswan, Egypt, for a discussion with Sadat, and we issued a joint statement emphasizing the need for full normal relations, a withdrawal by Israel from territories occupied in 1967, secure and recognized borders, and a resolution of the Palestinian problem in all its aspects. We still had no contact with the PLO, Jordan was equivocal about my efforts, and I expected Syria to oppose them if Egypt professed to speak for Arabs.

Begin was making military incursions into Lebanon and

announcements of further settlement activity, and Sadat responded by withdrawing all Egyptian visitors from Israel. I invited Sadat to meet with me at Camp David, and this precipitated a serious disagreement with all of my political, State Department, and national security leaders. My plan was to put Geneva aside, prepare as comprehensive an "American proposal" as possible, and try to induce Begin and Sadat to accept it. My advisers feared that such a meeting would fail, with dire consequences for the United States and the Middle East, but I was prepared to take the risk of failure.

When Sadat arrived at Camp David, he showed me a draft he had prepared for a speech to the National Press Club in Washington. He planned to say that he would discontinue any peace talks with Begin since he had offered everything Israel had wanted and the response was more belligerence and violations of U.N. resolutions, especially with the illegal settlements. After many hours of discussion, I convinced him that such a statement would make Egypt appear to be the party against peace and would be a violation of the previous commitments he had made to me of sustained cooperation. He finally delivered a fairly moderate speech, which expressed his concerns but remained positive.

During that time I was almost overwhelmed with energy legislation and other domestic issues and with international questions of nuclear arms control, the Panama Canal treaties, Rhodesia-Zimbabwe, and normalization of diplomatic relations with China, but my emotional involvement with the Middle East was preeminent. When Begin and Dayan came to visit me in March, I decided to "fish or cut bait." I got up even earlier than usual the morning of our meeting and wrote down six observations: they were not willing (1) to withdraw politically or militarily from any part of the West Bank; (2) to stop the construction of new settlements or the expansion of existing ones; (3) to withdraw Israeli settlers from Egypt's Sinai or leave them under U.N. protection; (4) to acknowledge that U.N. Resolution 242 applied to the West Bank–Gaza area; (5) to grant the Palestinians real authority or a voice in their own future; or (6) to discuss the issue of refugees. Dayan attempted to refute some of my statements, but Begin did not comment on their accuracy.

I was ready to withdraw from the Middle East peace issue entirely, and had a series of meetings to discuss the "six no's" with Israel's strongest American supporters. Most of them shared my deep concern about Israel's apparent rejection of any reasonable formula for peace. Strains continued between us and Israel during the following weeks, but I invited Begin to return to Washington to celebrate the thirtieth anniversary of the State of Israel. I asked two hundred rabbis to attend the ceremony, but twelve hundred people showed up at the White House gates and I asked them all to come in to the South Lawn. During my speech I reconfirmed my unfaltering support for Israel and announced the formation of a commission that would establish a memorial to Holocaust victims. Holocaust survivor Elie Wiesel became its chairman.*

As the weeks dragged by we continued to transmit nonsubstantive but generally negative messages between Israel and Egypt, and I met with both congressional and other strong supporters of Israel, who almost unanimously advised me, once again, to "stay as aloof as possible from direct involvement in the Middle East negotiations, which is a losing proposition." They emphasized that my administration and the Democratic Party were being severely damaged. Despite this, I sent both Secretary of State Cyrus Vance and Vice President Walter Mondale to the region. Nevertheless, they brought back nothing but discouraging reports. Sadat was meeting with the most radical Arab leaders to repair his fences with them.

While on one of our customary family visits to Camp David for the weekend, I discussed all these problems with Rosalynn, who was familiar with the basic issues. She recommended that we make one final effort, which might involve bringing both Begin and Sadat to this isolated place for full and frank discussions of all aspects of our peace proposals. I invited my top advisers to Camp David and shared this idea. No one thought we had much chance of success, but no one could think of a better alternative.

Keeping the entire process secret, I prepared long, hand-

---

* The superb Holocaust Museum in Washington is a tribute to their good work.

written letters to Begin and Sadat, and Cy Vance delivered them personally to the two leaders. Both responded positively, and on August 8, 1978, we made a simultaneous announcement of the plans. I also briefed congressional leaders and former presidents Gerald Ford and Richard Nixon, and the responses were cautiously positive. White House staff members were extremely critical of my firm decision to isolate the participants and exclude all news media during the discussions, which would be of indeterminate duration.

When we assembled at Camp David, it was obvious that Sadat was willing to accept almost anything I recommended, provided Israel would withdraw from the Sinai and, equally important, that the rights of the Palestinians would be honored. He was the most forthcoming of the Egyptian delegation. Begin, on the other hand, was more reluctant to make concessions than the other Israelis, and preferred to limit these peace talks to evolving some general principles, with the difficult details to be addressed later by cabinet officers.

I spelled out my most far-reaching proposals in a single document and began meeting with the two leaders in a small office in the cabin where Rosalynn and I stayed, with both Cy Vance and me taking notes. This proved to be a fruitless exercise, with Begin and Sadat personally incompatible and constantly having shouting matches as each issue was raised. They could not avoid resurrecting old grievances. After three days, I decided to keep them completely separate, and I spent the remaining ten days going from one leader to the other to resolve their differences, modifying almost word by word my "single document" as incremental progress was made.*

The breakthrough came during the penultimate day. Begin had taken an oath, before God, not to dismantle any existing Israeli settlement, and Sadat was demanding that all Jewish settlers had to leave the Sinai region. It seemed to be an insurmountable problem, and I was reconciled to failure. In preparation for our departure from Camp David, Begin requested that I personally sign photographs of us three leaders for each of his eight grandchildren. My secretary, Susan Clough, obtained the children's names, and I wrote "With love to —" on each of them above my signature. I decided to deliver the photos to Begin personally and found him polite but very stiff and unsociable when I entered his cabin. He thanked me, then looked down and read the inscriptions aloud, one by one. His lips trembled, and both of us wiped tears from our eyes.

I returned to my cabin, and soon thereafter his closest confidant, Aharon Barak,† came to suggest that we make one

---

* A detailed day-by-day description of the negotiating process is included in my presidential memoir, *Keeping Faith*.

† Barak was then attorney general but soon to be justice and then president of the Supreme Court of Israel for eleven years. Some legal scholars have called him the "world's greatest living jurist."

more attempt to resolve our differences. We finally agreed that the Israeli Knesset members would make the decision about Sinai settlers and would not involve the prime minister. Both leaders soon approved my final proposals.

The results exceeded all expectations, including written Israeli commitments to honor the provisions of U.N. Resolution 242, to withdraw their political and military forces from the West Bank and Gaza, and to grant the Palestinians "full autonomy" and a right to participate in the determination of their own future. Begin personally insisted on adding the word *full* to my original sentence (see Appendix 2). My additional proposed framework of a peace treaty between Israel and Egypt was accepted by both sides, with specific details to be negotiated in the near future. There was also a promise by Begin on a settlement moratorium during the time of implementing these terms. The Israeli Knesset soon approved the Camp David Accords by an 85–15 margin, and a comprehensive peace treaty was consummated in April 1979. This resulted in a prohibition of future combat between Egypt and Israel, mutual recognition, the exchange of ambassadors, withdrawal of Israel from the Sinai, and the use by Israeli shipping of the Suez Canal. No facet of this treaty has been violated during the succeeding three decades, but none of the promised rights of Palestinians (whose leaders refused to participate) has been honored.

• • •

During the last year of my term I was obsessed with an enormous legislative agenda and especially our American hostages being held by Iranian militants, so I couldn't put as much effort into implementing the Camp David Accords as was needed. But I was still attempting to marshal as much backing as possible for the peace agreements we had negotiated. An excerpt from my personal diary illustrates some of the encouraging support I received:

> In the afternoon I met with Saudi Prince Bandar, who brought a message to me from Crown Prince Fahd. They want to have a closer military relationship between Saudi Arabia, the United States, Israel, and Egypt. They want to help us in every way they can with our hostages, including sending Arafat to Iran. They were particularly eager to pursue the MidEast peace settlement by establishing a Marshall Plan type fund of about $20 billion, recognizing Israel, lifting the embargo against Israel, reestablishing ties with Egypt, provided Israel would carry out the spirit of the Camp David Accords and pledge to take care of the Palestinians and to withdraw from occupied

territories. Saudi leaders made it plain that they
were not talking about all occupied territory.
—December 15, 1979

At the same time, there were some disturbing indications
of significant opposition to the Camp David Accords and
Israeli-Egyptian peace agreements because of the concessions
Israel had made. Although Democratic presidential candidates in previous elections (including me in 1976) had been
able to count on overwhelming support from Jewish voters, I
received only 45 percent of their votes in 1980. Begin and his
successor, Yitzhak Shamir, favored peace between Israel and
Egypt, but some of their key political associates remained
strongly opposed to Israel's relinquishing control of Egypt's
Sinai. These naysayers included future prime ministers Benjamin Netanyahu and Ehud Olmert, with whom I later had
heated arguments about the subject.

Despite these disturbing omens, I left office believing that,
with President Ronald Reagan fully defending the Camp David Accords and the treaty with Egypt, Israel would soon realize its dream of peace with its other neighbors—a small
country no longer encircled by threatening nations.

4

REAGAN, BUSH I,
AND CLINTON, 1981–2000

Back home in Plains, I monitored events in the Middle East as closely as possible and, after realizing that this would be a low priority for President Reagan, began focusing on developments in the region as head of the new Carter Center. I was very pleased when both Anwar Sadat and Menachem Begin were awarded the Nobel Peace Prize and was delighted when Sadat and then Begin came to visit me in Plains to reaffirm their personal commitments to honor the promises they had made to each other. One of the greatest personal tragedies of my life and a severe blow to prospects for peace in the Middle East was the assassination of Anwar Sadat in October 1981.

There was another dramatic setback for the peace process in 1982, when Israel invaded Lebanon in response to terrorist attacks across its border. This military adventure turned out to be a disaster in several ways. Two hundred and forty-one U.S. servicemen stationed in Beirut were killed by a massive bomb explosion, which expedited the withdrawal of American forces from Lebanon. While Israel was leaving Beirut, there was a massacre of hundreds of civilians in two refugee camps, and later investigations in Israel revealed that the Israel Defense Forces had allowed Lebanese Christian militiamen to enter the camps and perpetrate the crime. Defense Minister Ariel Sharon resigned after the report was issued, and he was forbidden by a national investigating committee from serving in the same office in the future. (He would, however, serve as prime minister.) The PLO forces were required to leave Lebanon, but Israel continued to occupy a fifteen-mile-wide "security zone" in the southern region. Hezbollah grew in power and influence because of the Israeli occupation.

I used the resources of The Carter Center to stay informed and to probe for openings for peace in the region during the Reagan years and the first two years George H. W. Bush was in the White House. Usually accompanied by Rosalynn and a knowledgeable associate, Emory University professor Kenneth Stein, I visited the area several times, always with the knowledge and approval of the White House and State Department. After extensive conversations with the leaders of Israel, Jordan, Syria, Egypt, Lebanon, Saudi Arabia, and the Palestinians, I would report my observations to the currently serving national security adviser and to secretaries of state

George Shultz and later James A. Baker III. We kept meticulous records of the singular and often conflicting opinions of the foreign leaders, and in 1985 I wrote *The Blood of Abraham*, a book that presented these views as accurately and as clearly as possible.

Expulsion of the PLO leadership from Lebanon to Tunis, abandonment of Jordan's claims to the West Bank, and later preoccupation with the Iran-Iraq War all removed the Palestinian issue from the top consideration of Arab nations, and aroused an inclination among Palestinians to take independent action within the occupied territories to end the Israeli occupation. A movement known as the *intifada* ("shaking," or "waking up") began in 1987 and continued for several years. Although PLO leaders had access to many firearms, they restrained their use except against Palestinians believed to be colluding with Israelis.

Seventy thousand Israeli troops were deployed to confront mostly young people throwing stones. The human rights organization Al Haq reported that not a single Israeli soldier was killed during the first year of the intifada, and a total of only twelve during the first four years of the uprising. Israeli leaders announced that shooting into legs and breaking arms would be their primary response, but an Israeli spokesman acknowledged that 706 Palestinian citizens were killed during this same period. It was during the early months of this first intifada that the militant Palestinian Islamic organization known as Hamas was organized, with its charter, like that of the PLO, pledging to remove Israel from the Holy Land using violence if necessary.

President George H. W. Bush and Secretary of State James Baker brought a vigorous new approach to the Middle East region. At the same time, the PLO was indicating a willingness to move toward meeting Israeli requirements for negotiation. President Bush was a strong supporter of the Camp David Accords, and in May 1989, Secretary Baker announced to assembled members and supporters of the powerful American Israel Public Affairs Committee (AIPAC):

> Now is the time to lay aside once and for all the
> unrealistic vision of a Greater Israel. . . . Forswear
> annexation. Stop settlement activity. Reach out to
> the Palestinians as neighbors who deserve politi-
> cal rights.

Later, President Bush reminded the Israelis that East Jerusalem was occupied territory and not part of Israel. Agreeing with me and most of his predecessors, the president strongly condemned the Israeli settlements on Palestinian territory as illegal and key obstacles to peace. President Bush threatened to withhold a substantial portion of America's

$10 million of daily financial aid to Israel unless the settlements were stopped between Jerusalem and Bethlehem; $700 million was held back, and Prime Minister Yitzhak Shamir halted construction. Four hundred million dollars, the amount estimated to have been spent on the illegal settlements,* was still deducted.

Following the successful Gulf War launched against Iraq in January 1991, Bush and Baker turned their attention once more to the Middle East. Later that year Spain hosted a conference in Madrid, sponsored by Russia and the United States, which gave new vitality to the dormant peace process. The hosts invited Israel, Syria, Lebanon, Jordan, and the Palestinians to attend, but Israeli objections prohibited any Palestinians who were known to be associated with the PLO. Although the three days of talks did not produce any actual peace agreements, an organization was formed known as the International Quartet, comprising representatives of Russia, the United Nations, the European Union, and the United States. It would later become a forum for promoting peace in the Middle East. The Madrid conference also opened the way to many hitherto impossible discussions to continue in America, Russia, Germany, and ultimately in Norway.

---

* Construction of the same settlements was resumed when President Bush left office.

Most important, Norwegian mediators began secret negotiations between Israeli and PLO leaders, and both Yasir Arafat and Shimon Peres kept me informed. Rosalynn and I were in the desert in North Yemen in August 1993 when Arafat sent a message asking me to meet him in Sanaa. I flew down by helicopter, and he was beside himself with excitement as he revealed that a successful agreement had been reached and that Israeli leaders were on the way to Los Angeles to inform U.S. Secretary of State Warren Christopher that the peace talks had been held.

I quickly learned that the Oslo Agreement and its 1994 implementing agreement included some immediate actions but was primarily a framework for permanent relations between the two parties to be negotiated during a five-year interim period (to conclude by May 1999). The accords provided for the early creation of a Palestinian Authority to have responsibility for limited administration of the West Bank and Gaza and called for the withdrawal of Israeli forces from some parts of the occupied territories. This arrangement was supposed to last while a permanent agreement was negotiated concerning such issues as Jerusalem, Palestinian refugees, Israeli settlements, security, and borders.

Although delighted with this major step forward, I could see that, in effect, Arafat would have limited control over some communities in Palestine while Israel's military forces could still retain authority over any questionable area. During one of my visits to Israel, Rabin explained to me that he wanted Arafat to have all the authority he was able to exert effectively to control violence and to administer the mundane affairs of government—duties that were a headache for Israel. Rabin was equivocal about the much more difficult "permanent" issues but made it clear that all final decisions and the pace of implementation would still be made by Israel. Arafat was euphoric about his new status as the undisputed leader of the Palestinians, recognized by the world as he formed a new "government." He asked me again to begin preparations for monitoring elections to be held in the near future.

On September 9, 1993, Yasir Arafat notified Prime Minister Rabin that the PLO recognized the right of the State of Israel to exist in peace and security, acknowledged U.N. Security Council Resolutions 242 and 338 as the basis for peace, committed itself to a peaceful resolution of the conflict between Israel and the Palestinians, and declared that all outstanding issues relating to permanent status were to be resolved through negotiations. He declared that the PLO would help to guarantee "a new epoch of peaceful coexistence, free from violence and all other acts which endanger peace and stability." In return, Rabin gave official recognition to the PLO (not to a Palestinian Authority) as a legitimate governmental entity.

At first hailed as a major achievement, the Oslo Agreement was celebrated within a few days on the South Lawn of the White House with speeches and handshakes by President Bill Clinton, Yasir Arafat, and Yitzhak Rabin. I sat in the front row of spectators with American and other top dignitaries, while Rosalynn sat in the third row with the Norwegians who had negotiated the agreement. They were never mentioned during the ceremony. Arafat, Peres, and Rabin received the Nobel Peace Prize in 1994 for their achievement, and The Carter Center joined in sponsoring the erection of a large monument to the Norwegians on a hilltop in Oslo.

In the meantime, militant Israelis and Palestinians were rejecting the agreement. Ariel Sharon characterized it as "national suicide" and urged all Israelis to oppose its basic premises. Many Palestinians pointed out that the result was recognition of Israel by the PLO with no reciprocal commitment to a Palestinian state or agreement for Israel to withdraw from their land, except for Jericho and a few other communities within which Palestinians were granted self-rule.

With strong encouragement from President Clinton and Egyptian president Hosni Mubarak, an agreement between Jordan and Israel was signed about a year after the Oslo Agreement: the two countries ended the state of hostility and pledged moves to "a just and lasting peace." At least indirectly, this progress was the result of the Madrid conference, and, as an additional benefit, the number of nations worldwide that recognized Israel almost doubled, including India, China, and even a few Arab states.

The intensity of opposition to these fragile moves toward peace was demonstrated in November 1995, when an Israeli religious fanatic assassinated Prime Minister Yitzhak Rabin and was treated as a hero by some of his compatriots.

This is the excerpt from my diary:

> This was the day that Yitzhak Rabin was assassinated. It was a terrible blow, both to Israel and to the peace process—and to me. I have known him for 24 years, the first Israeli I ever met. He came to the governor's house to visit with us, and was the one who invited us to come to Israel in 1973. In S. Africa at the time, he returned home to be with us. . . . I came to know him well. He was extremely cautious, lacked any sense of humor, but was a bull dog once he made up his mind to do something. Shimon Peres was really the driving force behind the peace effort, but it took Rabin's leadership to get it done. In the evening, Clinton called to invite me to attend the funeral, along with Pres. Bush and a very large delegation of U.S. leaders—November 4, 1995

The next day I went to the funeral, and wrote:

> The outpouring of emotion in Israel was surprising. News reports said that 85 countries were represented at the funeral, including a number of Arab states. Hussein and Mubarak spoke, and Oman was there even though they don't have diplomatic relations with Israel. It was good to see some of my old friends, including Ezer Weizman, Shimon Peres, Aharon Barak, Ehud Olmert, and those from other countries. I also enjoyed being with George Bush, and joined him in our cabin for the flight over. . . . There is some general concern among Israelis that Peres will be too soft re the peace issue—not tough, reluctant, and cautious like Rabin.

Despite this tragedy, The Carter Center had made plans to monitor the Palestinian elections less than two months later, and we were thoroughly prepared for this assignment. A small group of distinguished leaders composed the electoral council, and the process was honest, peaceful, and fair. The only defect was severe restraints designed by the new prime minister, Shimon Peres, and other Israeli officials to minimize the number of Palestinians in East Jerusalem who were permitted to vote.

In fact, Israel refused to acknowledge that the Palestinian citizens had a right to vote locally, but rather claimed they were only expatriates mailing absentee ballots from East Jerusalem to be counted in the West Bank. Voting places were, therefore, limited to five post offices, four of them the size of mobile homes. Palestinians, of course, insisted that they were casting their votes on site, and we finally worked out a last-minute compromise by putting the slots on the top edge of the ballot boxes so that each ballot could be considered (by Israelis) as being put into a post office box horizontally or (by Palestinians) as being dropped into a ballot box vertically.

Arafat was elected overwhelmingly as president, and eighty-eight legislators were chosen. The Hamas leader Mahmoud al-Zahar had agreed earlier to refrain from violence during the election, but the membership was divided on whether to offer candidates. Some argued that if they participated in elections it would legitimize the Oslo Agreement, which they opposed because it accepted Israeli occupation of Palestinian territory. Arafat undermined those in Hamas who wanted to participate, and they did not, but after his victory he asked me to intercede with Hamas leaders and urge them to accept him as president in exchange for some positions in the government. My best efforts were unsuccessful, but Hamas did pledge not to interfere with the formation of the governing authority. Almost immediately, Israeli voters returned the Likud Party to power with Benjamin Netanyahu as prime minister, which spelled the end of the Oslo peace process. He adopted an adamant policy of rejecting three issues: negotiations with any preconditions, withdrawal from the Golan Heights, and discussion of Jerusalem.

There was some easing of tension when an international airport, later named for Yasir Arafat, opened in Gaza in 1998 and was heavily used by about two thousand passengers daily, and prospects for peace were raised with the election of Ehud Barak as Israeli prime minister in July 1999. In March 2000, Israel finally withdrew its forces from Lebanon, except for a few villages and adjacent land known as Shebaa Farms, which were claimed by both Lebanon and Syria. (Israel claimed it was Syria's.)

With minimal demurrals from Washington, Barak escalated the construction of settlements in the West Bank to an unprecedented level, but during the last year of his presidency President Clinton mounted a concerted effort for new peace agreements. For fifteen uninterrupted days in July 2000 and at other times he negotiated with Prime Minister Barak and PLO leader Arafat. Although there was no final signed agreement, the discussions contributed greatly to the clarification of many issues, and both sides said they accepted in principle Clinton's "parameters" (with Barak more specific than Arafat) concerning borders, Jerusalem, and other issues, but spelled out a number of exceptions. The Israeli and American leaders placed the blame for the continuing stalemate on Arafat.

In September 2000, after obtaining Barak's approval, Ariel Sharon visited the Temple Mount mosque with a large security contingent, implicitly affirming Jewish rights to the prominent site. Not surprisingly, violence erupted, and the Palestinian community launched a second intifada, more violent than the first.

Emphasizing national security, Sharon became the beneficiary of the violence that he had precipitated and was elected prime minister of Israel in March 2001. He was committed to rejection of the Oslo peace agreement and to the continuing expansion of settlements in the West Bank. The Gaza airport had been closed to traffic when the intifada began, and Sharon ordered the runway bulldozed, along with seventy Palestinian homes.

5

THE EARLY BUSH II YEARS, 2001–2005

As President Clinton left office, the key Middle East negotiators attempted to salvage some of the near agreements from the preceding peace efforts and initiated new talks at Taba, Egypt, the day after George W. Bush became America's president. Facing defeat for reelection by Ariel Sharon, Israeli prime minister Ehud Barak distanced himself from these negotiations, and he and Clinton announced that any agreements reached by him or Clinton on parameters would not be binding on their successors. He also declared a sustained freeze on implementing terms of the Oslo Agreement.

Although substantive negotiations between Sharon and Arafat seemed out of the question, it was still possible for the unofficial efforts at Taba to provide a foundation for future peace talks. Perhaps because the intense pressures were eased,

Map 3

Major Israeli
Checkpoints
Within the
West Bank

Mediterranean Sea

ISRAEL

WEST BANK

JORDAN

Jordan River

- Netanya
- Baqa
- Jenin
- Qabatiya
- Arraba
- Al-Zababda
- Maythalun
- Tulkarem
- Nablus
- Qalqilya
- Beit Furik
- Tel Aviv
- Salfit
- Birzeit
- Ramallah
- Al-Bireh
- Jericho
- Ashdod
- West Jerusalem
- East Jerusalem
- Bethlehem
- Surif
- Tarqumiya
- Sa'ir
- Hebron
- Dura
- Yatta
- Addahria
- Assamu'a

Dead Sea

Main roads
Green Line
Jerusalem municipality
Major checkpoints

0   5   10 miles
0   5   10 kilometers

N
W   E
S

there was more willingness on each side to be accommodating, and, with U.N. Security Council Resolution 242 as a framework, the participants made substantial progress concerning the crucial issues of borders, settlements, Jerusalem, and the Palestinian right of return. Also, the substantial differences that remained were clearly defined. There was a presumption that all of Gaza would be under Palestinian control, but a sharp dispute remained over whether and how much deviation there should be from the 1967 border between the West Bank and Israel. Sharon later agreed with me that Gaza and the West Bank would be linked by a safe passage. Sharon said that he preferred a rail corridor and a highway alongside, with security controlled by Israel and the trains to be operated by Palestinians.

It was decided at Taba and in subsequent discussions* that all settlements in Gaza and the West Bank would be vacated except for those in a small area near the existing border.† As agreed many years earlier by Begin and Sadat at Camp David, Jerusalem would be undivided, with Arab neighborhoods governed by Palestinians and Jewish neighborhoods as part of Israel. The city would be open and the capital of both nations, with holy sites controlled by the respective believers. There were still some unresolved questions concerning the exact delineation of these areas.

---

* All these discussions were unofficial, leading to the Geneva Accord.

† See Map 4 on page 66 and the Web site www.geneva-accord.org for text.

Implementation of U.N. Resolution 194 concerning the right of return was discussed, with the Israeli side demanding tight restraints on Arab refugees moving back into Israel. There was general agreement that the Palestinian state would be demilitarized or have limitations on its acquisition of arms. There were further discussions regarding control and use of airspace over Palestine and the rapidity of Israeli settlement withdrawal from the West Bank and the Jordan Valley. The presence of international peacekeeping forces was also considered. The final statements of the chief negotiators at Taba are a good indication of the positive spirit of this final effort.

Shlomo Ben-Ami (Israeli) said, "We made progress, substantial progress. We are closer than ever to the possibility of striking a final deal."

Saeb Erekat (Palestinian) said, "My heart aches because I know we were so close. We need six more weeks to conclude the drafting of the agreement."

Their joint statement: "The sides declare that they have never been closer to reaching an agreement and it is thus our shared belief that the remaining gaps could be bridged with the resumption of negotiations following the Israeli election."

• • •

A potentially momentous event occurred during the last week in March 2002, when all twenty-two members of the Arab League endorsed a peace plan at their summit meeting in Beirut. They offered to recognize Israel's right to exist in peace and to initiate diplomatic relations; Saudi King Abdullah stated that in trade and commerce they would treat Israel the same as they dealt with each other. The proviso was that Israel would comply with pertinent U.N. resolutions still endorsed by the United States and other nations (see Appendix 3). It is interesting to note that this proposal was adopted the following month by the Organization of the Islamic Conference (OIC), which includes fifty-seven nations (many non-Arabic). When the OIC reiterated its support in October 2003, the Iranian delegation expressed its full approval as it pledged to "use all possible means in order to explain and clarify the full implications of this initiative and win international support for its implementation."

Tragically, at almost the same time a suicide bomber killed thirty civilians in Netanya, Israel, and Prime Minister Sharon retaliated with a massive military attack on the West Bank, almost completely destroying and then isolating Arafat's headquarters in Ramallah.*

Violence escalated during the next months almost entirely

---

* From then until his final illness two and a half years later, Arafat was surrounded by Israeli forces and treated as a prisoner under house arrest.

within Palestine, with militants in Fatah, Hamas, and various other organizations known as Palestinian Islamic Jihad, al-Aqsa Martyrs' Brigade, and Popular Front for the Liberation of Palestine resorting to suicide bombing and using small arms, hand grenades, Qassam rockets, and homemade bombs. The Israel Defense Forces employed tanks, bulldozers, howitzers, and military aircraft including American-made F-16s, helicopter gunships, and drones. In the densely populated Gaza Strip, Israeli snipers were very effective firing from high towers. Using information from Palestinian informants, the Israelis were especially successful in the targeted killing of prominent leaders of the militant organizations. During the second intifada and before a Gaza truce was accepted in June 2008, reliable human rights organizations reported that 334 Israeli military personnel and 719 Israeli civilians were killed. There were 4,745 Palestinian fatalities, of whom 1,671 were assumed to have been militants. It is difficult to ascertain who among the Palestinians were active combatants, but 119 Israeli children and 982 Palestinian children were among the dead.

The hitherto dormant International Quartet (United Nations, United States, Russia, and the European Union) formed at the Madrid conference of 1991 was given new life in April 2003, when U.N. secretary-general Kofi Annan released the details of a plan for an independent, viable, peaceful, and democratic Palestinian state to exist side by side with a secure and internationally recognized state of Israel (see Appendix 4). The step-by-step process became known as the Roadmap for Peace with the final phase, then targeted for 2005, to include an end to the Israeli-Palestinian conflict, agreement on final borders and the status of Jerusalem, removal of Israeli settlements, solution of the refugee issue, and peace between Arab nations and Israel. Intermediate steps included the end of Palestinian violence, formation of a new Palestinian government through elections, Israeli withdrawal to pre-intifada lines following an immediate freeze on settlement activity, and economic recovery in the occupied territories.

The United States and Israel refused to deal with Palestinian president Arafat, and in 2003 Mahmoud Abbas (Abu Mazen), apparently approved by President Bush and Prime Minister Sharon, began serving as prime minister. He resigned after five months because of nonexistent peace efforts and conflicts with Arafat over reforming security forces. In May 2003, Prime Minister Sharon made the surprising statement that the "occupation" of Palestinian territories was "a terrible thing for Israel and for the Palestinians" and "can't continue endlessly." He endorsed the Roadmap but with debilitating reservations (listed in Appendix 5) and embarked on a plan of unilateral withdrawal from Gaza while retaining control of its borders, coastline, and airspace. Responding to virulent criticism from conservative political allies, Sharon's top aide explained that the move was designed to "stop the peace process" and delay the establishment of a Palestinian state until after all terrorism was ended.

It was good that Sharon finally recognized the futility of occupying Gaza, but his unilateral withdrawal rather than one negotiated with the Palestinian Authority proved to be a serious strategic miscalculation. It weakened the Palestinian moderates who wanted to negotiate peace with Israel and strengthened the militants, who claimed that Israel withdrew only because of their violent resistance. It also led many Israelis to conclude that Palestinians would not accept Israel even if it withdrew, thus leading Israelis to believe they should remain in the West Bank. A negotiated withdrawal would have strengthened the peace process.

We at The Carter Center monitored developments in the Middle East closely and were pleased that Israeli justice minister Yossi Beilin and Palestinian Authority minister Yasser Abed Rabbo, both longtime peace negotiators, continued to build on the results of the Taba talks for an unofficial agreement. This accord was highly specific and courageously addressed the key issues of borders, Jerusalem, and the right of Palestinians to return to their homeland. We were given detailed briefings on progress and attended some of the negotiating sessions, and I gave the keynote speech in Geneva in November 2003, when the final results were revealed. About two hundred Palestinians and an equal number of Israelis attended the event. Since the proposal was balanced and completely compatible with international law and the Quartet's Roadmap, there were public endorsements from Prime Minister Tony Blair, Presidents Jacques Chirac, Bill Clinton, Nelson Mandela, and Lech Walesa, plus Nobel Peace Prize laureate John Hume and about eighty other world leaders. The Bush administration did not take a position but indicated its tacit approval when Secretary of State Colin Powell received the two chief negotiators for a thorough briefing. Predictably, Sharon and the more militant Palestinian leaders condemned the proposals. Copies were distributed to all available mailboxes in the Holy Land, and subsequent public opinion polls revealed that a majority of citizens in both Israel and Palestine approved the Geneva Accord.

In addition to Israel's multiple settlements and checkpoints, a serious obstacle to accommodation between Israelis and Palestinians is the "security fence," "separation barrier," or "apartheid wall" being built mostly in the West Bank. The various names illustrate vividly the controversial nature of the structure. It is necessary to understand this important new feature on the Middle East landscape because it has become a major symbolic and practical impediment to a peace agreement.

Map 4

Geneva Accord
Recommended
Land Swaps,
2003

Nazareth•

Jenin•

Netanya•

Nablus•

Mediterranean Sea

Tel Aviv•

WEST BANK

N
W • E
S

Ramallah•

Jerusalem★

ISRAEL

•Hebron

Jordan River

JORDAN

Dead Sea

GAZA STRIP

Gaza•

Rafah•

•Beersheba

EGYPT

NEGEV

Green Line

Annexed to Israel

Annexed to Palestinian Areas

0   10   20 miles
0   10   20 kilometers

Such a barrier was first proposed by Yitzhak Rabin in 1992 with the announced purpose of deterring suicide bombers who were attacking Israeli civilians. Rabin ordered a wall to be constructed around Gaza two years later, along the internationally recognized boundary between Egypt, Israel, and Palestinian territory. This would be following the accepted dividing line with the presumption that any future construction between Israel and the West Bank would follow recognized borders. The International Court of Justice ruled that Israeli defense along this boundary was legal and proper.

Later, in 2003, Prime Minister Sharon made a basic change in the barrier's location and character. He began to clear a path about two hundred feet wide almost entirely on Palestinian land, in the center of which would be a network of impenetrable fences in more sparsely populated areas and concrete walls up to forty feet high where more protection was considered necessary. A common design is to have three steel fences, with stacks of barbed wire for the two outer ones and a higher fence with intrusion detection equipment in the middle. Patrol roads are provided on both sides of the middle structure, and an anti-vehicle ditch is located on the Israeli side plus a smooth dirt strip for "intrusion tracking." All gates are either kept locked or controlled by Israeli soldiers.

I had heard descriptions of the barrier but could not envision its enormity until we visited the area to monitor the election in 2005. As a farmer, I was especially disturbed by the wide swaths bulldozed through Palestinian streets, yards, gardens, fields, and orchards to make way for the barrier itself and by the routing to enclose choice Palestinian land.

About one-fifth of the wall is at or alongside the Green Line, but in most places the barrier is built entirely in the West Bank, penetrating as much as thirteen miles into Palestinian territory to encompass existing and growing Israeli settlements and desirable land and building sites not yet confiscated. When completed as planned in 2010, it will be about 435 miles long, and it may connect to the north and south ends of the Jordan River valley, occupied by Israel. This will completely encircle that portion of the West Bank remaining in Palestinian hands (see Map 5). In many places the barrier prevents Palestinians' access to their fields, grazing lands, schools, or places of worship. Some cities, including Bethlehem and Qalqilya, are almost completely surrounded by the high wall.

In a 2004 decision, the International Court of Justice declared construction of the wall *in Palestinian territory* "contrary to international law." When Israelis claimed that the exact pre-1967 boundary could not always be followed because of large buildings or topography, the court suggested that in those cases it be built on the Israeli side. The United Nations stated in a 2005 report: "The land between the Barrier and the Green Line [pre-1967 border] constitutes some of the most fertile in the West Bank. It is currently the home for 49,400 West Bank Palestinians living in 38 villages and towns."

The legal rulings were ignored by the Israeli government, and a state of animosity and violence continued as Israel Defense Forces commanders declared that this Palestinian territory was now a closed military area, and that every person over twelve years of age was required to have a permit to continue living in their homes. Other West Bank residents could enter only with a special visitor's pass. There are numerous lawsuits being decided by the Israeli high court, and some minor modifications to the exact route have been ordered to minimize harm to local citizens when Israeli security cannot be proven a factor.

Public opinion about the barrier is as divided as the land, with a strong majority of Israelis believing that it enhances security and marks the eventual West Bank boundary. Palestinians maintain that other factors have reduced violence, that the same results could have been achieved with the wall on the international border, that the barrier cannot stop hand grenades, rockets, or mortar attacks, and that its main purpose is to take their land and is therefore a major impediment to peace. The international community, including the International Court of Justice, United Nations, International Red Cross, all European nations, the World Council of Churches, Amnesty International, Human Rights Watch, B'Tselem, and other human rights organizations, is almost unanimous in condemning the placement of the barrier as illegal. In 2003, President George W. Bush said, "I think the wall is a problem. . . . It is very difficult to develop confidence between the Palestinians and Israel with a wall snaking through the West Bank." Later, he wrote to Prime Minister Sharon that the wall "should be a security rather than political barrier, should be temporary rather than permanent and therefore not prejudice any final status issues including final borders, and its route should take into account, consistent with security needs, its impact on Palestinians not engaged in terrorist activities."

The bottom line, however, is that construction of the fence, or wall, continues. Israeli leaders have maintained that the barrier is not permanent and may be moved or removed when Palestinians can guarantee the safety of Israeli citizens. Palestinians respond that the real purpose of the barrier is to move the international border eastward to confiscate their land and therefore deter progress on any kind of peace agreement.

Yasir Arafat died in November 2004, and we at The Carter Center were asked once more to monitor an election two months later to choose his successor. We had a joint National Democratic Institute–Carter Center observer delegation of eighty members from fifteen nations and enjoyed a good working relationship with other observers from the European Union. We all recognized that the Palestinian people lived under Israeli political and military occupation—a situation unlikely to change until good-faith peace talks could follow the Palestinian Authority's willingness and ability to control acts of violence against Israeli citizens, or at least demonstrate a sincere and determined effort to do so. Our hope was that the choice of a moderate leader and the subsequent election of parliamentary members would provide a strong and respected government that could meet these requirements.

Normally there were very restricted movements of Palestinians through about five hundred Israeli checkpoints and the dividing wall, but we hoped to see the roadways opened for the election period. There were also severe limitations on voter registration, campaigning, and voting in East Jerusalem. Of the 150,000 eligible voters living in the city, fewer than 6,000 would have Israeli permits to cast ballots near their homes. These few could still vote only in the five post offices, where Israelis could claim, as in 1996, that the "absentee" ballots were being mailed outside. Approximately 140,000 other registered voters were expected to refrain from voting or leave the city and cast their ballots in neighboring communities. Many would-be voters were intimidated by posted warnings that they would lose their dwelling rights. No Palestinian officials or observers would be allowed to enter the polling places, all of which were manned by Israeli postal employees. Any campaigning was also forbidden within East Jerusalem. One candidate (Mustafa Barghouti) was arrested after meeting with our observer delegation when he attempted to seek votes near the Lion's Gate.

When I arrived in Tel Aviv in January 2005 to participate in this effort, I met once again with Ariel Sharon. From my diary:

> The prime minister and I exchanged memories of our joint experiences during the past 26 years, and I thanked him for his positive influence on Prime Minister Begin while I was negotiating as president at Camp David and later in Washington and Israel to conclude the peace treaty with Egypt. Sharon promised that the West Bank check points would be manned by soldiers but would not impede traffic and that military forces would be withdrawn from major cities during the election period. He also assured me that he had enough votes in the Knesset to overcome any opposition to withdrawing the 8000 Israeli settlers from Gaza. Knowing him, I did not doubt his promises.— January 6, 2005

Our delegation heard presentations from three candidates prior to Election Day, but it was almost a forgone conclusion that Prime Minister Mahmoud Abbas (Abu Mazen) would be elected. The superb work of the Central Election Commission ensured that, throughout Gaza and most of the West Bank, the electoral process would be conducted properly and without violence. In East Jerusalem, however, where the commissioners were denied jurisdiction, apparently deliberate incompatibility between the voter lists and ID cards prevented any Palestinians from casting their ballots until 2 P.M., when I finally resolved the issue just three hours before the polls closed by using our observers to approve voters.

Abbas received 62 percent of the votes and was quickly sworn in as president. When I met with him the next day, he said that he was eager to begin peace negotiations with Israel and America, and that he had accepted all facets of the Quartet's Roadmap but that Sharon had rejected more than a dozen of its key provisions. At that time, elections for parliamentary members were scheduled for July, but they were postponed to permit the withdrawal of settlers from Gaza and also because Hamas decided, for the first time, to field party candidates for the legislative body.

With the election of a new Palestinian leader, it seemed to me that dramatic events were impending in the region, and I decided on my way home in January 2005 to collect excerpts from my voluminous personal diary and other sources for a book on the subject. I felt strongly, as I had in 1977, that the time was ripe for another major effort to negotiate the terms of a comprehensive peace settlement and that the United States would have to play a key role.

I decided to confine myself to conditions within the occupied territories and not to any events in Israel, and I had plenty of material for the text. While monitoring the Palestinian elections, our Carter Center observer teams had been required to learn as much as possible about the occupied territories, and their detailed reports to me had been combined with the personal notes that Rosalynn and I had taken. Collectively, our observations covered the entire region, concentrating on those sites in Gaza and the West Bank where altercations or disputes had been prevalent or where issues were most sharply defined. We had become acquainted with many of the candidates and had analyzed their differing campaign techniques and appeals to the voting public. I studied the nuances of all the peace proposals as they had been revealed and was intrigued by the specific points discussed for many months while final elements of the Geneva Accord were consummated.

The still unscheduled parliamentary elections would give us a chance to observe the growing competition between the Fatah Party of Abbas and Arafat and the more militant Hamas. Our long-term observers maintained a presence in the Holy Land as various dates were considered for the upcoming elections, which were finally set for January 2006. During more than sixty-five troubled elections around the world, it had been our policy to remain completely neutral among the competing candidates and to learn as much as possible about all of them. We would be constrained in this case, however, because the National Democratic Institute had been our partner in the previous election and the relationship had continued. As it received U.S. funds, it could not have direct contact with Hamas or its candidates before the election, and we complied.

6

---•◆•---

WITHDRAWAL FROM GAZA
AND ITS AFTERMATH

Ariel Sharon overcame all obstacles to removing the eight thousand Israeli settlers from Gaza in August and September 2005 and from four small "illegal" settlements in the West Bank. Substantial cash awards were made to the settlers, and new dwellings were guaranteed in the nearby Negev region (where Sharon lived) and in other parts of Israel or the West Bank. Armed troops removed by force the few who protested most strenuously.

It had long been clear from the prime minister and many other Israeli leaders that Gaza had little religious or strategic importance to them, the area having been controlled even during biblical times by Philistines (unconquered by King David or King Solomon). In many ways it would be a relief, and many Israelis would be quite happy, if Egypt would reas-

Map 5

Palestinians Surrounded, 2008

Nazareth•

Jenin•

Netanya•

Nablus

Mediterranean Sea

Tel Aviv•

WEST BANK

Jordan River

JORDAN

Ramallah•

Jerusalem★

ISRAEL

•Hebron

Dead Sea

Gaza•

GAZA STRIP

Rafah•

•Beersheba

EGYPT

NEGEV

	West Bank Boundary
	Completed Wall (July 2008)
	Proposed Wall Route
	Area of Planned Israeli Control
▲	Permanent Settlements from the Olmert Plan

0   10   20 miles

0   10   20 kilometers

sume control of the small, densely populated, and trouble-some area. Gaza was about thirty-five miles from the nearest point in the West Bank and completely enclosed by a high wall penetrated by a few gates, only two of which were opened, at times that were chosen by the Israelis. Although it was a unilateral decision by Israel, Hamas claimed political credit for the settlers' withdrawal.

Hamas had contested and won a number of municipal offices during earlier elections and, in general, had governed well. It had worked to clean up the communities' streets and empty lots and had enforced local laws; there were no allegations of corruption and no excessive intrusion of religion into the secular lives of citizens. This time it had candidates for all parliamentary seats except the six set aside for Christians.

As election time for the 132 parliamentarians approached, Israeli and Fatah leaders urged that the contests be postponed because of the likelihood of some Hamas victories, but the United States, espousing democracy, insisted that elections be held as scheduled. Some of the public opinion polls showed Hamas candidates receiving as much as 35 percent of the total votes. To dampen support for Hamas, there were threats to Palestinian voters that even this modest involvement in government would preclude the initiation of peace talks between Israelis and Palestinians (already absent for three and a half years) and could terminate hundreds of millions of dollars in humanitarian aid from the United States, Europe, and other sources that had been channeled through the Palestinian government.

Fatah, the party of Arafat and Abbas, was vulnerable because of its cumbersome bureaucracy and well-known corruption. Another major factor was that both Israel and the United States had ignored Abbas as an acceptable negotiating partner, and therefore Palestinians questioned his ability to negotiate a peace agreement with Israel. Many of Fatah's old-line leaders had been replaced by younger candidates, who were mostly loyal to Marwan Bin Khatib Barghouti, an activist serving a life sentence in Israeli prisons.

Barghouti is one of the most intriguing players in the Middle East political drama and had announced his candidacy in December 2004 to oppose Mahmoud Abbas as Arafat's successor. He was still a prisoner, having been one of the few Palestinians tried in a civilian court instead of a military tribunal. He had returned from exile in Jordan to be elected to the Legislative Council in 1996 and espoused the peaceful establishment of the approved Palestinian state. As secretary-general of Fatah in the West Bank he had conflicts with Arafat when he condemned human rights violations and the corruption that permeated their party. Barghouti claimed to have renounced attacks against civilians but maintained that he had a duty to support armed resistance to the occupation within Palestine, and he was finally arrested by the Israeli army in April 2002.

Barghouti refused to present a defense and asserted that his trial was illegitimate because he was a legislator, arrested in an area over which Israel had no authority, and his transfer from the occupied territory to Israel for trial violated the Fourth Geneva Convention. He was accused of thirty-three counts of murder during the first and second intifadas and found guilty on five hazy charges involving Israeli Druze soldiers. Sentenced to five life sentences plus forty years, he remained extremely popular among Palestinians of all parties and respected by many political leaders in Israel and within the international community.

He withdrew as a presidential candidate to avoid splitting Fatah any further and, still a prisoner, was reelected to the Legislative Council in January 2006. His release from prison has been urged by supporters of both Fatah and Hamas, by members of the European Parliament, and by several Israeli parliamentarians. Shimon Peres promised during his campaign for president of Israel to pardon Barghouti, but this has not yet happened. In Palestinian demands for prisoner exchange, his name has topped the lists, despite the fact that he is potentially more popular than any other leader and could compete with them for future political roles.

Perhaps Barghouti's most notable contribution as a prisoner has been joining with fellow inmates representing Hamas and other factions in proposing a plan for Palestinian reconciliation. Not only did it spell out the framework for a coalition government between Hamas and Fatah, but it also called for comprehensive peace negotiations with Israel. There is little doubt that many of his proposals will be utilized by any Palestinian unity government of the future. We noticed that Israeli leaders wanted his views to be publicized when they permitted Barghouti to be interviewed by *Paris Match* and other international periodicals. He told leading Israeli political leaders that "it is possible for Israel and the Palestinians to reach a final-status agreement along the lines of the Geneva Accord." With impeccable revolutionary credentials and respect from many Israelis and from Palestinians of both major factions, and being an advocate for Palestinian unity and peace with Israel, Marwan Barghouti could play a key future role in promoting harmony in the Middle East.

Facing persistent opposition from Benjamin Netanyahu and other right-wingers to his unilateral withdrawal from Gaza and portions of the West Bank, Sharon announced in November 2005 the formation of a new party named Kadima (meaning Forward). Key founders were Shimon Peres and Tzipi Livni, plus Ehud Olmert as Sharon's heir apparent. Its platform declared that the Israeli nation has a historic right to

the whole of Israel but will give up portions for exclusive occupation by Palestinians to maintain a Jewish majority within
the retained homeland. Two adjacent states for two nations
would be formed in stages, as Palestinians dismantle terror
organizations, collect firearms, and implement security reforms in compliance with the Roadmap.

Prime Minister Ariel Sharon suffered a massive stroke in
January 2006 and was unable to continue the duties of his office, and Ehud Olmert became the acting prime minister. Although The Carter Center had long-term observers deployed
in Palestine, the election itself was still uncertain because of
the continued debate about whether Hamas candidates and
potential victors would be recognized as legitimate. Washington finally prevailed in demanding that the election be held,
and we election monitors moved to our posts.

There was some conjecture within our group about the
unswerving commitment of President Bush to a democratic
election between the two major Palestinian factions, and the
most obvious opinion was that it had been the influence, and
misunderstanding, of Natan Sharansky's book *The Case for
Democracy*. Earlier, the president had announced that he had
read the book and given copies to his top advisers. Bush said
publicly, "If you want a glimpse of how I think about foreign
policy, read Natan Sharansky's book." He had then invited the
author to the White House, consulted with him, and included
some of the book's premises in his second inaugural address.

Although Sharansky had called for a Palestinian society that would be free and without fear, it is unlikely that he was contemplating a free election with unlimited participation by Hamas candidates.

On our arrival in Tel Aviv, Rosalynn and I first met with Ehud Olmert, whom we had known for more than twenty years. He and I had had many arguments (and some agreements) since he was a young Likud candidate, and I had come to appreciate his intelligence, political acumen, personal ambition, and strong will. We knew he would be a formidable leader of the new Kadima Party, and he assumed the official title in April, after Sharon had been incapacitated for a hundred days. Olmert made it clear to us that he would continue Sharon's policies and would conduct peace talks with Abbas, but only after all radical Palestinian groups were completely disarmed. I asked if a sincere and determined effort with substantial results would be adequate, and he smiled and said, "No, I mean one hundred percent." We both knew that this would be a hopeless prospect if he took his pledge seriously.

The following morning, I addressed the Herzliya Conference, an important forum for Israeli and international leaders. (This was the group to which Sharon first announced his intended withdrawal of settlers from Gaza.) Even though I recognized the very conservative nature of the audience, I decided to express my opinions frankly and briefly and then to answer questions. I thanked them for the friendly reception but commented that the questions received more applause than my answers.

Just to illustrate our operating procedures in election monitoring projects, let me note that we met with key players Álvaro de Soto (U.N. coordinator for Middle East peace), Israeli foreign minister Tzipi Livni, Labor Party leader Amir Peretz, Shimon Peres, Quartet special envoy James Wolfensohn, a spokesman for Hamas (not candidates), candidates of Fatah and independent parties, Yossi Beilin and others who had orchestrated the Geneva Accord, members of the Central Election Commission, leaders of several other international election observer groups, and Palestinian president Mahmoud Abbas and his top aides.

Although Abbas expressed confidence in a Fatah victory, he was obviously distressed at having been bypassed or ignored in the peace process. He pointed out that the Palestinian economy was in a shambles and had accumulated a $900 million deficit. While demanding that he maintain complete order among all the disparate Palestinian factions, Israel imposed restraints that precluded the training and equipping of his security force, with only 10 percent of its personnel being armed or equipped even with communications equipment.

On Election Day, Rosalynn and I visited more than two dozen polling sites in East Jerusalem and its outskirts, Hebron, Ramallah, and Jericho. It seemed obvious to us and other observers that the election was orderly and peaceful.

Hamas assumed a moderate position during the campaign, omitting any mention of violent action and calling only for "the establishment of an independent state whose capital is Jerusalem." Almost all our observers detected a clear preference for Hamas candidates even in historically strong Fatah communities, but we were still surprised at the extent of the Hamas victory. Although receiving only 43 percent of the popular vote, Hamas candidates won a clear majority of parliamentary seats (74 of 132 members). Fatah was so divided that it often ran two or more candidates for the same seat, while Hamas had only one, who received all the votes of supporters. Public opinion surveys showed that Palestinians voted for Hamas because many believed that democracy would be enhanced if the two key parties shared or alternated power and not because they wanted a conflict with Israel.

Abbas announced plans for his Fatah government to resign, and I decided to remain for an extra day or so to assess the situation and to discuss the future with key leaders. I returned to Ramallah and found President Abbas willing to stay on as president during the three years remaining in his term but in a quandary about how to deal with the Hamas victory, the formation of a new government, the near bankruptcy of his government, and uncertainty about Israeli policies. He was justifiably proud of the admirable election process. Hamas leaders expressed their desire to form a peaceful unity government with Fatah and the smaller independent parties, but Abbas was under great pressure from Jerusalem and Washington not to cooperate with them. I urged him to reconsider. This was something of a mirror image of the situation ten years earlier, when Fatah had prevailed and I had tried unsuccessfully to induce Hamas to accept the newly elected government.

Abbas informed me that there were not enough funds available to meet his February payrolls for teachers, police, nurses, and other public workers, and that any reduction in financing because of the election results would be disastrous. He felt that one of the major factors in the voting had been his apparent ineffectiveness in being ignored by Israel and the Quartet leaders. He reminded me that there had been no opportunity for a Palestinian leader to participate in peace talks for almost four years. In our center's Ramallah office, I learned from some Hamas spokesmen that their key political leaders were in Gaza and that there was some question about their being able to come to Ramallah or anywhere else in the West Bank to form the elected government and to administer Palestinian affairs in the future.

This was hard to believe, so I called the Israeli prime minister's office and was told that no Hamas party member would be given a pass to change location anywhere within the occupied territories. This would prevent the results of the election from being implemented and could provoke an intense reaction and perhaps permanent divisions and violence among

Palestinians, regardless of party. I informed the U.S. consul general, who said he had not heard of this policy, and he promised to inform the ambassador, the State Department, and the White House.

It was obvious to me that a peaceful unity government could be formed and that it was a prerequisite to any substantive move toward peace between Palestinians and Israel. I knew that Hamas had not expected to win the election, and that neither Israel nor the United States had been prepared for this outcome. All sides needed to have some time, at least until Hamas could make a choice between accepting the basic provisions of the Oslo Agreement or rejecting its unexpected opportunity to participate in government. I was tired and in a quandary about what could be done.

On the flight back to Atlanta I decided to attend the meeting of the International Quartet, scheduled to convene in London. I was at home only one day, prepared my remarks, and returned. Although visitors had not previously been welcomed, the assembled representatives of the United Nations, United States, European Union, and Russia agreed to allot twelve minutes on the program to me. They listened politely while I described the election and appealed to these leaders to find a way to honor the results, permit travel of elected parliamentarians, influence Arab nations to honor any future peace agreement acceptable to the Israelis and Palestinians, enforce U.N. Resolution 242, promote full human rights for Palestinian citizens in their own homeland, and ensure that the Palestinian Authority had adequate funds to meet its basic needs. I added, "I am convinced that Israelis and Palestinians want a durable two-state solution. Recent polling from Hebrew University and Palestinian pollsters indicates that more than 63 percent—almost two-thirds—of Israelis and Palestinians support basic parameters that offer a reasonable alternative for both sides. The Quartet is the only group that can help to realize this dream."

I then attended the press conference a few minutes later and noticed that no changes had been made to the minutes as drafted before the participants assembled. All my points had been ignored, and, in effect, Hamas was precluded from participation and there would be no unified Palestinian government.

After this failure to see a potential voice established to speak for all the Palestinians, I decided to maintain a more permanent presence for The Carter Center, so we retained our election headquarters in Ramallah with a small staff. This gave us a helpful but limited insight into current developments among Israelis and Palestinians.

7

SPASMODIC PEACE EFFORTS,
LONG OVERDUE

A major event after the Palestinian election, and one that added a new dimension to the Middle East conflict, was the capture of three Israeli soldiers and the Israeli response. In June 2006, a group of militants tunneled under the wall around Gaza and attacked an Israeli military outpost. A brief gun battle followed that left two Israeli soldiers and three Palestinians dead. Corporal Gilad Shalit, an Israeli soldier, was captured. This event would increase tensions and open years of difficult negotiations, through Egyptian mediators, for his release in exchange for a large number of prisoners held by Israel.

There was a much more serious result two weeks later, when Hezbollah demonstrated its support for the Palestinians by attacking two vehicles containing Israeli soldiers near the

Israeli-Lebanese border. Two were killed, three wounded, and two others taken captive, either seriously wounded or dead. The Israeli cabinet authorized "severe and harsh" retaliation and followed with an invasion of southern Lebanon and a massive bombing attack on many parts of the country, while Hezbollah launched several thousand missiles into northern Israel.

After thirty-three days of intense combat during which more than a thousand Lebanese and 159 Israelis died, the U.N. Security Council adopted Resolution 1701, which called for cessation of hostilities, Israeli withdrawal of its forces from Lebanon in parallel with deployment of Lebanese and U.N. soldiers in southern Lebanon, the disarmament of militia groups, full control of Lebanon by its government, and no Hezbollah forces south of the Litani River. A tenuous cease-fire has been the only tangible result as Israel continues to occupy parts of Lebanon (or Syria), Hezbollah remains armed, and no forces have challenged Hezbollah's influence in south Lebanon.

Although comparative casualty figures indicated a great Israeli victory, the Israeli army's failure to overpower Hezbollah's militia resulted in a general perception that the relatively small number of Lebanese militants had prevailed. Hezbollah launched wild celebrations while an investigative committee was established in Israel to determine who among top officials was most to blame. With major contributions from Iran and some Arab countries, Lebanese homes were rebuilt and other war damage repaired, with Hezbollah claiming credit for the benevolent assistance.

In February 2007, King Abdullah of Saudi Arabia orchestrated an agreement in Mecca between Hamas and Fatah, but it was based on a vaguely worded text. Animosities between the two groups, along with U.S. and Israeli political and economic pressures on President Abbas, were successful in abbreviating the life of the unity government that was formed.

Israel arrested and imprisoned forty-one elected Hamas parliamentarians who lived in the West Bank and ten prominent citizens who had been proposed by Hamas as cabinet members. This removal of Hamas officials made possible the formation of an interim government in the West Bank, with nonpartisan Salam Fayyad as prime minister and a non-Hamas cabinet. This acting government rules by decree until new elections can be held. This still left an unresolved struggle for Gaza. There were a number of truces declared and broken between leaders of Hamas and Fatah, while Israel continued to bombard the area in response to Qassam attacks. Hamas declared its rule over the northern city of Beit Hanoun and occupied the Fatah headquarters. After intense combat, the Fatah forces were overcome, and Hamas assumed military and political control of Gaza in June 2007.

This meant that Palestine was now divided into two parts, with President Mahmoud Abbas and an interim government in the West Bank and with Prime Minister Ismail Haniyeh, an elected parliamentarian, as the titular leader in Gaza. The ultimate leadership of Hamas, however, was a group of politburo members in Damascus, Syria, headed by Khaled Mashaal. Israel, of course, retained actual control of the West Bank.

In the meantime, the violence of the second intifada continued, with Israel conducting regular nightly raids in the West Bank against suspected militants. B'Tselem reported 1,787 Palestinians killed in the West Bank by the Israel Defense Forces and 41 by Israeli settlers between September 2000 and September 2008. Qassam rockets were launched from Gaza into the nearby Israeli village of Sderot, and retaliatory Israeli strikes against Gaza cost 2,974 Palestinian lives, while 580 Israelis were killed. The need for peace talks was obvious.

A new opportunity to share responsibilities and involve The Carter Center came in July 2007 with the formation of The Elders, unveiled by Nelson Mandela, Sir Richard Branson, human rights activist Peter Gabriel, and others. I was asked to serve, along with former U.N. secretary-general Kofi Annan, Mary Robinson (former president of Ireland and later U.N. high commissioner for human rights), Gro Brundtland (former prime minister of Norway and head of the World Health Organization), Archbishop Desmond Tutu, Graça Machel (Mandela's wife), Muhammad Yunus (founder of Grameen Bank, which gives microloans to women), Fernando Henrique Cardoso (former president of Brazil), Ela Bhatt (women's activist from India), and Lakhdar Brahimi (former Algerian foreign minister and senior diplomat of the U.N.). None of us was any longer involved in partisan politics. Aung San Suu Kyi was a symbolic choice, although she had been in prison or house arrest in Myanmar almost continually since 1989 and was unlikely to be released in the near future.

What the Elders had to offer was our collective experience and reputation plus complete independence from the political constraints of nations or international organizations. Our first choices for frank assessment were the Middle East and Darfur, in the Sudan. Tutu, Machel, Brahimi, and I made a visit to Sudan and Darfur in September and October 2007. We subsequently issued a report of our findings and followed up with letters, editorials, and media interviews. The Carter Center also remained involved in completing a national census and preparing for Sudanese elections scheduled for 2009.

We decided that Kofi Annan, Mary Robinson, and I would compose the delegation of Elders to the Middle East. The first planned date for our visit to the region was October 2007, but we ultimately postponed it until April 2008 because of the Annapolis conference and then a trip by President George

Bush to the region in January. Robert Pastor, American University professor and interim codirector of the Elders, and a small staff made a preparatory tour of Israel, the West Bank, Egypt, Syria, Saudi Arabia, and Jordan.

We sent letters to Prime Minister Olmert and other leaders informing them of our plans, and, once again, Pastor made the requisite tour to prepare for our visits with key players. We acquired visas, arranged for transportation, and continued to assess political developments in the area. Everyone understood that the Elders had no authority and would not mediate or play any role in the negotiations among the United States, Israelis, and Palestinians. Our plan for the mission was to consult with all the major players in the Middle East disputes, probe for possibilities for reconciliation, and then make a public report that would delineate the options available for others to make tangible moves toward a peace agreement.

We found most Palestinians eager for the Elders to play a role, with Israeli government officials skeptical but peace groups and human rights organizations in the country supportive of our producing a helpful analysis of the overall process. Egyptian leaders suggested additional roles for the Elders: to encourage the U.S. administration to lead and to induce the "spoilers"—Hamas, Hezbollah, and Syria—to desist from violence during peace negotiations and either remain neutral or supportive of the outcome. We might also give support to more moderate groups that were not involved in the direct negotiations, let these outsider voices be heard, and encourage acceptance of any negotiated agreements.

A few facts seemed obvious to us concerning the Israeli-Palestinian issues, the most notable being the inescapable need for some kind of Hamas involvement. Governing about 1.5 million people in Gaza and with support from an unknown but substantial number in the West Bank, this group could launch a new wave of violence or at least obstruct the implementation of any kind of peace deal. It was increasingly difficult for President Abbas to ignore Israel's isolation of Gaza and the intense economic restraints and military attacks on its Palestinian inhabitants, many of whom were members of Fatah and still on the Palestinian Authority payroll. Both Israel and the United States had declared publicly that any Palestinian unity government would mean the end of the ongoing peace talks unless Hamas was willing to forgo violence, accept previous peace agreements, and acknowledge Israel's right to exist in peace. We would explore possible ways to overcome this obstacle.

Both Ehud Olmert and Mahmoud Abbas were seen to lack political strength, with each side claiming that the other's weakness was the main problem. The Israelis believed Abbas to be sincere but unable to deliver an agreement, and the Palestinians suspected that Olmert would delay any serious decisions for fear of breaking his government coalition, which was dependent on support from religious parties that objected to substantive discussions of settlements, Jerusalem, or the right of return of Palestinians to their former homeland. Both assessments were correct. The Palestinian spokesmen were placing some faith in the international community to make sure their concerns were addressed. Many on both sides also wished that the United States would take the lead, draft a reasonable agreement, and induce both sides to accept it.

Since the Bush administration failed to assert any such leadership, there was a growing sense that U.S. influence in the peace process was waning. There was no participation by Americans—or anyone else—in the crucial private talks between Abbas and Olmert. The Palestinian president told Jordanian news media that resumption of the armed struggle against Israel might be necessary. We were certain that our mission would do no harm.

We Elders observed very closely the much-publicized tour of President George Bush through the Middle East in January. There was no discernible positive impact on peace for Israel or its neighbors. Once again, the Israeli government publicly rejected a settlement freeze, the number of roadblocks continued to increase, and economic restraints on Gaza were tightened. After meeting with Prime Minister Olmert in Jerusalem and being quite cautious about prospects for 2008, President Bush went to Ramallah and predicted that a Middle East peace treaty would be completed during his term in office.

While with the Palestinians, Bush outlined a balanced peace proposal that dealt with the core issues. He called for the return of or just compensation for Palestinian refugees and a "viable, contiguous, sovereign and independent" Palestinian state, based on the 1949 armistice line, with "mutually agreed adjustments." He declared that it was time "to end the occupation that began in 1967," when Israel had seized the West Bank and Gaza. He did not make a proposal regarding Jerusalem but called its status "one of the most difficult challenges on the road to peace." His other comment regarding the pervasive Israeli settlements pleased his Palestinian hosts: "Swiss cheese isn't going to work when it comes to the outline of a state."

After visiting the Church of the Nativity in the now walled-in city of Bethlehem, President Bush said that he hoped to see a Palestinian state without Israeli walls or checkpoints and that his peace quest was motivated by his "belief that there is an Almighty, and a gift of that Almighty to each man, woman and child on the face of the Earth is freedom."

Mohammed Shtayeh, the Palestinian official in charge of rebuilding the West Bank, said, "This is what the Palestinian people have been waiting for. The President has always talked about his vision for a state, now he's talking about ending the occupation." The Israeli response was not as favorable. "What's come out of this trip is just warm rhetoric. Anyone who expected more than that is going to be disappointed," said Yossi Alpher, a key Israeli adviser during the 2000 Camp David peace talks. "What is [Mr. Bush] prepared to do about it? Nothing, other than rhetoric, and he leaves tomorrow."

It seemed that Alpher was right. Bush still refused to consider a strong mediation role by the United States, and there was no indication that the U.S. government would take any specific action to break the stalemate that existed in the peace talks between Israel and the Palestinians.

Except for his comments in the West Bank, it seemed that throughout his tour of the region the president's primary emphasis was on Iran, not the peace process between the Israelis and Palestinians. In an interview with news media in Jerusalem, Bush stated, "Part of the reason I'm going to the Middle East is to make it abundantly clear to nations in that part of the world that we view Iran as a threat, and that the NIE [National Intelligence Estimate] in no way lessens that threat, but in fact clarifies the threat." This comment was pertinent because key persons in his administration and in Israel were waging a propaganda war against Iran because of its enrichment of nuclear fuel. In a major setback, U.S. intelligence services had announced in December that Iran had abandoned its nuclear arms program in 2003. When this report was leaked to the public, it aroused dismay among the hawks in the United States and Israel, who maintained that Iran was a major threat to peace, with some advocating preemptive military strikes. President Bush and Israeli leaders condemned "misinterpretations" of the report.

There was a pervasive belief in the Arab world that the extended occupation of Iraq had greatly enhanced Iran's influence in the region, and that the administration's lassitude regarding peace efforts indicated an abandonment of Palestinian rights. Some of America's key Arab allies had begun reaching out to Iran to an unprecedented degree. The previously scorned Iranian president Mahmoud Ahmadinejad had been invited to speak before the Gulf Cooperation Council— originally formed by Sunni leaders specifically to counteract the Iranian threat—and Saudi king Abdullah had welcomed him to make the Hajj religious pilgrimage to Mecca. This was the first time an Iranian president had participated in either event. There were reports that Egypt and Iran were discussing the resumption of diplomatic relations, after twenty-eight years of estrangement.

Public opinion polls in the Arab world revealed that the United States was seen as a greater threat than Iran, and a successful peace effort in Palestine could be the most important factor in improving its citizens' opinion of America.

To illustrate the restraints on Israeli negotiators, in mid-January, four days after President Bush left Israel and on the last day of his regional tour, a conservative faction in Prime Minister Ehud Olmert's coalition pulled out of the government because they thought the core issues—Jerusalem, right of return, and borders—were on the agenda for further peace talks. The leader of the faction told a news conference, "Negotiation on the basis of land for peace is a fatal mistake." This left Olmert with only 67 seats in the 120-seat Knesset, and the ultra-Orthodox Shas Party also threatened to withdraw its 12 lawmakers if there should be any compromise over Jerusalem.

As the peace process remained bogged down, President Bush shifted his public assessment of the prospects for a breakthrough. During the time between his Middle East visit and the State of the Union address on January 20, he changed his appraisal from "I believe it's going to happen, that there will be a signed peace treaty by the time I leave office" to an effort "that defines a Palestinian state by the end of this year."

Even more than before, it seemed that an independent assessment of peace prospects in the region was needed.

8

HOW CLOSE IS ISRAEL TO
ITS MAJOR GOALS?

After the Bush visit in January 2008, it seemed that the Israelis had less incentive to compromise. They had a superb and proven military force, were powerful and secure behind the separation wall, and had more than two hundred settlement communities in the West Bank, a network of exclusive highways, more than six hundred checkpoints constraining Palestinian movement, and an iron grip on Gaza. The inherent weakness of the Palestinians, exacerbated by the divisions between Hamas (in Gaza) and Fatah (in the West Bank), made it difficult for Mahmoud Abbas to take strong action to alleviate their plight. Also, any real pressure from Washington or any other outside source on peace talks was highly unlikely.

Stating that its action was in response to mortar fire, Israel closed all border crossings into Gaza on January 17, cutting off most of the food and other humanitarian supplies that normally met the daily needs of its 1.5 million inhabitants.* The loss of fuel caused the electric power generators to shut down, depriving the people of light, heat, and sewage disposal pumps. Thousands of Palestinian women demonstrated at the Rafah gate, which opens into Egypt, demanding access to health care, and were pushed back by Egyptian guards. People in the territory had been cut off from the outside world for seven months, since Hamas had seized power in Gaza.

Christopher Gunness, a spokesman for the U.N. agency in charge of Palestinian refugees, said that sealing the Gaza crossings "can only lead to the further radicalization of a depressed and demoralized people." A spokesman for Abbas, Nabil Abu Rdeineh, told the Associated Press the decision was calling into question any further peace talks: "No one can proceed with negotiations when the situation is like this." The Palestinian Authority threatened to suspend negotiations with Israel, and the Arabic daily *Al-Quds* reported that Abbas was suggesting he might resign.

Three days after President Bush's State of the Union address, Gazans set off explosives at seventeen points along the seven-mile wall on their Egyptian border, and bulldozers leveled the debris to permit passage of motor vehicles. A massive

---

* Before the January 2006 election, about 500 truckloads entered Gaza each day. Between June 2007 and June 2008, the average was 64 truckloads daily. After the cease-fire of June 19, the daily rate increased to 129 truckloads.

stream of about a half-million Gazans—one-third the total population—crossed the border and returned peacefully to their homes with purchased goods. In stores and shops in nearby Rafah, Egyptian shoppers stood aside to permit their neighbors to buy food, fuel, and other supplies. The Egyptians still imposed travel restrictions, with Palestinians not permitted to go farther than El Arish, twenty-five miles from Rafah.

Hamas police directed traffic, while Egyptian border guards stood aside. Israeli officials announced that they had no control over the situation and that Egypt had full responsibility "according to the signed agreements." Public statements from Jerusalem and Cairo made it clear that Israel wanted Egypt to assume responsibility for Gaza and that Egypt rejected the idea. Palestinians in both major factions agreed, seeing the potential transfer of Gaza to Egypt as a threat to their ultimate unification into a state.

American diplomats in the region informed me that Mahmoud Abbas was making public statements that mirrored overall Palestinian concerns, but that he privately considered the breached wall to be beneficial to Hamas. The overall assessment was that Hamas hoped to see a joint monitoring of the border by Egypt and Hamas. Israel, of course, still controlled Gaza's access to the sea and airspace and the only land crossing through which major supplies could be delivered. As Egypt slowly closed the wall again, Khaled Mashaal announced from Damascus that he had accepted an invitation from Egyptian president Mubarak to resume unity talks in Cairo, but Mahmoud Abbas repeated his stance that he would not meet with Hamas until it apologized for its June 2007 "coup" in Gaza and handed power back to the Palestinian Authority.

Although neither Egypt nor Israel would agree to have Hamas in charge of a border crossing, Prime Minister Olmert announced that Israel would no longer disrupt the supply of food, medicine, and necessary energy into Gaza and intended to prevent a "humanitarian disaster" there. In order to reestablish control over the border and prevent another outbreak, President Mubarak ordered that the quantity of consumer goods going into El Arish and Rafah be restricted. After all this furor, the status quo ante prevailed, with Israel still in charge.

Assessing the situation, Daniel Gavron, a fervent Israeli Zionist and author, published an interesting editorial in *The New York Times* that described the situation in the Middle East as many other people assess it. Although not professing to be speaking for most Israelis, he claimed "astonishing success" for the Zionist movement, pointing out that "virtually the entire world, including all the Arab nations" have accepted "the existence of the State of Israel in 77 percent of the land of Israel." He added, "We have won, but we are refusing to accept the result. It is as if the captain of a team winning the World

Cup, a triumphant Olympic sprinter or a victor of Wimbledon were to say: 'No, no. There has been a mistake. I didn't win, I lost. My victory is an illusion.'"

Gavron went on: "The Palestinian Hamas, which rules Gaza, refuses to recognize Israel, but even that movement seeks a long-term truce, which is tantamount to de facto recognition. Far more significantly, Fatah, the official Palestinian leadership, is negotiating peace with Israel. The member states of the Arab League, headed by Saudi Arabia, are on record as recognizing Israel within its pre-1967 borders. The world's only superpower, the United States, is solid in its support of Israel under any conceivable president. The other four permanent members of the United Nations Security Council, the European Union and the overwhelming majority of the members of the United Nations all recognize pre-1967 Israel."

He added, "For any 'two-state solution' to work, we would need to conduct a complete withdrawal from the West Bank. Even so, the success of the Zionist enterprise would be astounding. What we should not be doing is what we are doing now: besieging and blacking out Gaza, killing and arresting dozens of Palestinians in the occupied territories every month, and constructing walls and fences between us and our neighbors. . . . To cower behind a wall is to demonstrate again our loser mentality at a time when we have, in fact, won. The political settlement that the world is begging us to reach is the only way to ultimately stop the violence between us and the Palestinians."

In both Washington and Jerusalem, the primary focus remained on Iran's potential threat, while most Arab governments saw increased militancy in the region as a result of a lack of progress in resolving the Palestinian issue. When Jordan's King Abdullah II addressed a joint session of the U.S. Congress in March 2007, his emphasis was on the peace process. "The wellspring of regional division, the source of resentment and frustration far beyond, is the denial of justice and peace in Palestine." This portion of his speech was barely mentioned in the U.S. news media.

The cycle of violence between militants in Gaza and the military forces of Israel continued. The bombardment of the nearby town of Sderot by Qassam rockets from northeastern Gaza—an average of two per day—instigated retaliatory bombing and rocket strikes by Israel. A plan was approved by the Israeli government to construct shelters within homes that would protect people from the rockets, and news media reported a substantial increase in those Israelis calling for an armed invasion of Gaza. However, such an invasion would be very costly and make it practically impossible for Abbas to continue peace talks with Olmert. We Elders decided to put Sderot on our itinerary when we visited Israel.

While this confrontation continued, several Arab leaders, perhaps reacting to the breach of the Gaza wall, threatened to withdraw their previous offer to normalize political and economic relations with Israel. Prominent Arab news media declared that the two-state solution for peace was dead because of Israel's apparent unwillingness to withdraw settlements from the West Bank or deal with the questions of Jerusalem and the Palestinians' right of return. A single nation was a longtime goal of some leading Israelis, along with a mass exodus of Arabs from the occupied area, but neither Egypt nor Jordan was willing to consider accepting a large number of Palestinians who might pour across their borders.

Palestinian Authority President Mahmoud Abbas, now governing only 60 percent of the Palestinians (those living in the West Bank), was becoming increasingly discouraged about the prospect of progress toward a peace agreement. According to Palestinian negotiator Saeb Erekat, Abbas told visiting Vice President Dick Cheney that the United States needed to support talks mediated by Egypt seeking an agreement with Hamas "to have the Israeli government accept a reciprocal cease-fire." But Israel would not officially acknowledge taking part in any such talks, and both sides publicly reserved the right to attack the other at any time. The bloody stalemate would continue.

. . .

There was an important legal milestone at the end of March, when the Israeli Supreme Court rendered a decision giving approval to what had been a de facto exclusive road system in Palestine for Israelis. This was described by the Association for Civil Rights in Israel as "the onset of legal apartheid in the West Bank." This network of roads restricted to Israeli vehicles was not new, but the issue had never before been approved by the high court. Originally built on privately owned Palestinian land with about half its length in the West Bank, the highway in question, Route 443, was the main road connecting Modiin with Jerusalem, nineteen miles away. Mostly four-lane, it had been constructed more than twenty years earlier when the Supreme Court had supported the claim of the Israeli army that its primary purpose would be for the use of the local Palestinian citizens. Israeli settlers had increasingly used the highway, and finally Israel blocked Palestinian access to it.

Along with its decision to approve exclusive Israeli use, the court directed that the army would give a progress report after six months on its building separate roads within Palestine with, perhaps, compensation for the Palestinians. Some conservative Israelis maintained that there was no ethnic discrimination, since Arabs who are Israeli citizens could use the highway. These Arab citizens, of course, are not settlers in the West Bank and had little use for the road, and their travel from Israel into Palestinian areas was restricted.

Limor Yehuda, an Israeli civil rights lawyer, said that the Supreme Court's 1982 ruling had specifically stated that if the point of the road was primarily to serve Israelis, then it could not be built. Yet now, she added, "The state is essentially aiming to safeguard the convenience of the service road for Israelis who commute from Tel Aviv and the central plains to Jerusalem and vice versa."

There were other explanations of the high court's ruling from a political point of view. *The Jerusalem Post*'s Dan Izenberg explained that international law and Israeli court decisions were unambiguous on the fact that the road should serve primarily Palestinians rather than Israelis but that the court was in a delicate political position just then because of growing public discontent with it over other issues. He wrote, "The High Court in this case cannot stray too far from the interests of the Israeli public, especially at a time when it has more than its share of enemies. The court knows that Israelis who rely on Highway 443 would not easily accept a ruling that causes them such inconvenience."

For the thirty thousand Palestinians who lived in the surrounding villages, lack of access to Route 443 had been a constant source of difficulty. In one village, A Tira, fourteen taxis had permits to travel a portion of the road during daylight hours, but locals said that had not eased the burden much. Each morning, a crowd gathered at the blocked entrance to A Tira, waiting for the Israeli soldiers to open a gate so they could take one of the taxis to Ramallah, the capital of the West Bank.

"Ten days ago, my brother had a heart attack and we had trouble transferring him to a Ramallah hospital," lamented Said Salameh, fifty-one, a taxi driver who had a permit to use the road. "When the gate closes at night, we can't move outside the village." Sabri Mahmoud, a thirty-six-year-old employee of the Palestinian Authority, agreed. "I am always late to work because of this," he said. "Our life is controlled by the opening hours of the gate. You feel like you live in a cage."

Legal commentators in Israel stated that the most distressing aspect of the decision was that by giving Route 443 to Israelis and barring Palestinians from it, Israel was protecting its citizens not from terrorism but from traffic—granting them an alternative to the crowded main Jerusalem road.

President Mahmoud Abbas broke off peace talks with Israel, and Secretary of State Condoleezza Rice hurriedly announced a visit to the region, to include meetings with Egyptian leaders and then to shuttle between Olmert and Abbas. The State Department reminded reporters that four simultaneous tracks had been established at Annapolis: (a) final status issues including Jerusalem; (b) easing security restraints and Jewish settlements in Palestine; (c) improving the Palestinian economy; and (d) greater involvement of the Arab nations. There was no evident progress on any of the efforts, and the United Nations reported an actual increase in roadblocks. Public opinion polls in both Israel and the West Bank showed that an overwhelming majority of those surveyed believed peace talks were being conducted only for political posturing.

We Elders monitored all these developments in the Palestinian area and were increasingly concerned about the sustained bloodshed and lack of any progress toward peace. Our most significant political question was our prospective meeting with leaders of Hamas. Israeli restraints on Gazans were increasing the popularity and influence of Hamas, and some distinguished American political leaders, including former national security advisers Zbigniew Brzezinski and Brent Scowcroft, and Lee Hamilton, former chairman of the House Foreign Affairs Committee and current director of the Woodrow Wilson International Center for Scholars, advised President Bush that "a genuine dialogue with the organization [Hamas] is far preferable to its isolation." At the same time in Israel, former heads of Israel's three intelligence services, Ami Ayalon of Shin Bet, Ephraim Halevy of Mossad, and Shlomo Gazit of military intelligence, expressed support for direct talks with Hamas. A Haaretz-Dialog public opinion poll conducted in March revealed that 64 percent of Israelis favored direct negotiations with Hamas, even including 48 percent of respondents from the hawkish Likud political bloc. All these comments and advice were immediately rejected by government leaders in the United States and Israel but strengthened our decision to meet with both Hamas and Syrian leaders.

Prime Minister Olmert was unable to engage in substantive negotiations as his coalition partners repeated a threat to pull out of the government if he should begin final-status talks on the formation of a Palestinian state. On March 17 he announced that Israel had the absolute right to continue expanding existing settlements and building new ones, especially around Jerusalem, despite objections from Washington or anywhere else. According to news reports, he also told King Abdullah II of Jordan that the talks between himself and Abu Mazen would not lead to any positive steps forward on the issues of settlements, Jerusalem, or final borders. In fact, in March, responding to intense pressure from right-wing participants in the coalition government, the government of Israel announced approval of one thousand more homes to be built in Palestinian territory in and around Jerusalem. Ariel Atias, the Shas minister of communications, said, "I am happy that wisdom prevailed."

In the West Bank, more roadblocks had actually been created since Annapolis, and there were now 50 percent more than two and a half years before. Each checkpoint created additional hardship for the Palestinians. For instance, the ten thousand residents of Azun now found their town almost completely isolated, with main streets blocked and frequent and unpredictable curfews that prevented citizens from going shopping and workers returning home at night. The community is near an Israeli settlement, and some Palestinians had violated prohibitions against using the connecting roadways. News reporters observed a group of Israeli soldiers in the center of Azun, who ordered all residents to return home and all outsiders to leave. One of them announced, "The village is closed."

It is very difficult for outsiders to envision the situation in Gaza. Its population was 80,000 before 1948, when 200,000 refugees came to the small area. About three-quarters of the present population are registered refugees, with more than half of them living in eight extremely crowded camps. Shortly before our planned visit to the region, Amnesty International and other human rights organizations reported that in Gaza, 80 percent of the people were dependent on food aid, 40 percent were unemployed, and 95 percent of industrial operations were suspended.

To assess the prospects for a comprehensive peace in the region, the situation in Lebanon and Syria would have to be understood, but our more immediate need was to comprehend more fully the stalled efforts to secure a peace agreement based on a two-state accommodation in the Holy Land. It was obvious to us that, along with Syria, Hamas must be involved. These were the opportunities being considered for our Elders' mission, with no prospect that any other entity might be willing to address them all. Although Hamas leaders made it known that they would welcome an agreement with Israel that included a cease-fire in the West Bank and Gaza and an exchange of prisoners, we knew that any such bilateral deal would be seen as strengthening Hamas and weakening Mahmoud Abbas—contrary to the desires of Israel, the United States, and many Palestinians. Our assessment would have to be carefully balanced.

9

A SEARCH FOR INFORMATION

After weeks of delay, Prime Minister Olmert replied to our letter that this would not be the best time for us Elders to visit because of the upcoming sixty-year birthday celebrations for Israel, which would attract a number of other foreign visitors. We responded that we would come ahead as planned and needed only a brief courtesy call with him and talks with a few of his cabinet members.

We had a telephone conference call to finalize our travel plans, and it was a disappointment to me when the Elders decided, in effect, to postpone our trip until there was approval from Israel. In fact, we had never expected for it to be politically possible for any Israeli leader to approve our entire mission, including meetings with Hamas or Syria. All plans had been completed, appointments made with political and private leaders, and I had set aside time for the trip. I was in a quandary and finally decided, with the encouragement of the other Elders, to carry out the same planned mission on behalf of The Carter Center.

I used key phrases from the Elders' previous public statement for my announcement of the mission:

> With deep concern about the long-standing conflict in the Middle East and an equally strong wish for peace . . . We plan to undertake a comprehensive analysis of the interlocking Middle Eastern conflicts . . . listen to all parties, and meet with leaders from governments, civil society, and key groups that influence the conflict in an attempt to understand their various perspectives. At the end of the mission, we will prepare a report for the public to help people understand the urgency of peace and what is needed to secure it. . . . We will also meet and begin to work with groups that will reinforce the efforts by the government of Israel and the Palestinian Authority to negotiate a peace agreement based on a two-state solution. . . . We genuinely hope that our efforts to learn from each of the parties can contribute to peace.

It was now less than three weeks before we needed to be in Israel to commence our Middle East tour, and I already had a full schedule. I was leaving in three days for scheduled visits to Ghana and Nigeria regarding our center's health programs, and immediately thereafter we would be in Nepal to monitor a crucial election.

As has always been my custom when planning foreign travel, I had notified the State Department three months earlier and received the necessary travel approval for the entire trip. This time, though, because of the sensitivity of some visits, I decided to speak personally to Secretary of State Condoleezza Rice. She was traveling in Europe, and her Middle East deputy returned my call. I described in detail our plans to visit Israel, the West Bank, Egypt, Syria, Saudi Arabia, and Jordan and meeting with Hamas leaders. He cautioned me about possible danger in Gaza, and I told him that I had already decided to meet the Gaza Hamas leaders in Cairo and others in Damascus. It was a pleasant conversation, with no negative or other cautionary comments.

It was very difficult to understand what was going on within the general framework of the peace talks. We studied with great care the balanced and constructive statements made by President Bush and Secretary Rice at Annapolis and during their visits to the West Bank, which were quite compatible with the Quartet's Roadmap and the previously stated policies of the U.S. government. At the same time, there had been a marked retrogression during the last few months in the observable measures of progress in the West Bank, notably the number of new settlements and checkpoints, extension of the separation wall into the West Bank, stagnation of the Palestinian economy, and new restraints on granting visas to college students.

My wife, Rosalynn, our son Jeff, and I arrived in Israel after an exciting and successful mission to Nepal to monitor a crucial election that was designed to end a twelve-year civil war, create a new democratic republic, and give "untouchables" and other marginalized people their first role in the political and social life of the country. We were met in Tel Aviv by Robert Pastor, Hrair Balian, the newly arrived director of our center's conflict resolution program, and Steve Solarz, who served as a senior member of the House Foreign Affairs Committee for eighteen years and was one of the leading supporters of Israel in Congress.

Since Israel had declined to welcome the previously planned visit by three of us Elders, I expected a similar reaction when The Carter Center filled this role. Sure enough, all my offers to meet with ministers of the government were rejected, but we were informed on arrival that my family was invited to meet with President Shimon Peres. I didn't wish to cause Prime Minister Olmert any embarrassment, so we quietly transferred the time set aside for official meetings to additional sessions with elder statesmen and business leaders. Luckily, in a democracy like Israel there are numerous sources of information from private citizens who are experts on government policies and attitudes, and they could give us thorough briefings on official Israeli policies, many of which were already well known to me and to the general public.

Rosalynn, Jeff, and I had a very pleasant and congenial exchange with Shimon Peres, but later one of his aides reported incorrectly that it had been a harsh confrontation and that I had been condemned and berated about our travel plans. Our next meeting was with Noam and Aviva Shalit, the parents of the young Israeli soldier who had been held for about eighteen months by the Palestinians in Gaza. We pledged to do our best to learn about his condition, perhaps to obtain a letter from him, and to aid in his release.

After a much-needed rest, we began the next day with an extended briefing by Israeli public opinion researchers on their latest findings. The general summary was that Jewish citizens in Israel were fairly satisfied with the status quo, had little confidence in the peace negotiators on either side, chose not to be informed about the plight of the Palestinians, and, surprisingly, were much more concerned about the "right of return" than about withdrawing from settlements or sharing Jerusalem with Palestinians.

We then visited Sderot, a town of about twenty thousand that was traumatized by the random but deadly rockets launched from Gaza. The streets, playgrounds, and other public places were empty, and about three thousand residents had moved away. We looked at nearby Gaza from a hilltop and then had a long discussion with Mayor Eli Moyal and several outspoken citizens in his office. He said that there were two ways for a government to protect its people: by diplomacy or military action—and the Israeli government was doing neither for his town. We promised to explore possibilities for a cessation of the rocket fire and then toured the Barzilai Medical Center in nearby Ashkelon. Trauma victims are brought there from Gaza and Israeli communities, with no distinctions in treatment between Jews and Arabs. Prospective patients from Gaza, however, had to prove at the checkpoint that their families were not associated with Hamas. Long involved in mental health programs, Rosalynn was especially interested to learn that debilitating psychological injuries (stress disorders) were far more prevalent than physical wounds.

That afternoon we met with families of the two soldiers captured by Hezbollah, who had received no indication of whether they were still alive. We then had an intriguing discussion with about a dozen Israeli "elders," who had held major positions in intelligence, government, and the military or had experience in previous peace negotiations. At the end of the session, I felt that most of them approved of our pending visit with Hamas and Syria. Later in Ramallah we talked with Palestinians who were involved in various peace discussions and then met in our office with diplomats from about fifty nations who were assigned to Israel or the Palestinian Authority. This was a good opportunity for us to gain the perspective of many nations.

The most emotional event of our entire trip was a meeting with young Palestinians, mostly of college age. The description of their lives and of family members was distressing, and their determination and hope for a better life brought tears to our eyes. Even though born and raised in Ramallah, Jericho, Bethlehem, or Nablus, they and their families often had citizenship rights taken away just because they might have visited or studied elsewhere. Many relatives had been imprisoned for years because of some nonviolent political activity.* The students, here and in Gaza, either were denied permission to study abroad or were afraid that foreign travel would result in their loss of citizenship. Some of them hinted at the possibility of a third intifada.

We had an extensive discussion with Salam Fayyad, a

---

* Including women and children, the Israelis were holding 11,600 prisoners, and about 25 percent of the entire Palestinian population had been arrested.

highly respected economist, trained at the University of Texas, who serves as prime minister of the interim Palestinian Authority. A forceful and independent thinker, he expressed hope for reconciliation between Hamas and Fatah. The prime minister gave us some suggestions for our meetings with Hamas leaders. He emphasized, quite emotionally, "Unless America stops the Israelis from expanding settlements there can be no peace." He almost shouted, "Not one more brick!"

We had a discussion with about a dozen Palestinian "elders" from both political parties. I embraced Eyad Sarraj, a psychiatrist from Gaza and the leader of a human rights group, a former prisoner who had been released when I interceded with Arafat. He and Rosalynn had also cooperated in his work as head of the leading mental health clinic. This became a worldwide news story when some thought, incorrectly, that he was close to Hamas. After other meetings during the afternoon, we returned to East Jerusalem for a session with the Israel-Palestine Business Council, a group attempting to demonstrate that trade and commerce between the two entities are both possible and profitable. Its successes had been limited, at best.

Our first meeting the next day was with Avigdor Lieberman, leader of Yisrael Beiteinu (meaning Israel Our Home). His small party had recently withdrawn its support from

Olmert's Kadima. Lieberman believes that Jews and Arabs should be completely separated and advocates giving Arab-Israeli towns near the border to the Palestinians and requiring any Arabs who wish to remain Israeli citizens to take loyalty tests, while some more distant Israeli settlers in the West Bank would return to Israel.

The role of the United States in the occupied territories is very important, and we were grateful to obtain a briefing from General Keith Dayton, U.S. Security Coordinator, and his multinational staff. They were able to answer only a few of our questions because there were many taboo subjects they were forbidden to discuss. He had been in the region for two and a half years, was obviously dedicated and competent, and had to accommodate changes in his assigned duties each time there were different circumstances on the ground. His major current project was to train a small professional security force of Palestinians to provide whatever security services in the West Bank the Israelis would relinquish. The first community chosen was Jenin, a site of violence during the early days of the second intifada. This experiment is being watched closely as a possible precursor for other sites where Palestinians can replace Israelis in maintaining order.

Our next meeting, with Deputy Prime Minister and Minister of Industry and Trade Eli Yishai, was quite interesting. He is the leader of Shas, a conservative religious group of a dozen Knesset members who are dedicated to peace—and holding on to all of Jerusalem. He was supportive of our mission and asked us to help arrange a meeting for him with Hamas leaders in order to help orchestrate the release of Corporal Shalit. He was the only member of the Israeli cabinet who met with me.

That evening we heard reports from representatives of more than a hundred organizations in Israel and Palestine whose members are publicly promoting peace based on the general formula of two states living side by side. We found them disappointed with the lack of substance at Annapolis and the slow pace of negotiations since then. Almost universally, they doubted that there would be any progress in the ongoing talks between Prime Minister Olmert and President Abbas or the parallel discussions between Israeli foreign minister Tzipi Livni and Palestinian negotiator Ahmed Qurei (Abu Ala). As expected, they all supported our mission, and I advised them to concentrate their diverse efforts around a common acceptance of the Geneva Accord.

Our last stop before flying to Egypt was Hadassah Medical Center, where wonderful work is being done with an important emphasis on harmony between Israelis and Arabs. The patients as well as the staff included Jews and Arabs from both Israel and Palestine.

• • •

In Cairo we had an intriguing session with Egyptian chief of intelligence Omar Suleiman, who is in charge of all the relations with Hamas. Through him, the United States and Israel are able to negotiate with Hamas while publicly denying any relationship. He answered our questions with no restraint and was extremely impressive. His position gives him, I believe, unique insight into the intricacies of Middle East political and military affairs.

During a congenial luncheon with President Hosni Mubarak and his wife, Suzanne (old friends), we discussed former times and how much Egypt has been blessed by the peace treaty with Israel. Not engaged in warfare, having had its land and oil wells returned, and being a special friend of the United States, Egypt is thriving. With the president and prime minister, I urged acceptance or at least tolerance of nonviolent political parties in coming elections.

Instead of going to Gaza, which would have required a two-day round trip by automobile from Cairo, I had asked President Mubarak to arrange for the Hamas leaders to meet us in Cairo. Our session with Mahmoud al-Zahar, Sayeed Siam, and Ahmed Yousef went on for more than three hours. Well briefed by Minister Suleiman, we made full use of this time. Knowing that we would find the real authority in Damascus, I discussed ideas for a cease-fire in Gaza, the exchange of prisoners, and interim steps to permit reconciliation with Fatah and the holding of Palestinian elections. They maintained that, with a cease-fire, they could persuade the more militant factions to cease launching Qassam rockets into Israel. When I requested a letter from Corporal Shalit to his parents, they would not acknowledge that he was still in Gaza, which made me wonder if the soldier was still alive. It was an interesting discussion and helped prepare us for the meeting in Damascus with Khaled Mashaal, to whom they referred all final decisions. In this and other discussions, Pastor and Congressman Solarz played a crucial role.

The next morning we flew to Damascus, where we first met with President Bashar al-Assad, Foreign Minister Walid Mualem, his deputy, Faysal Mekdad, and other officials. They seemed pleased with a recent visit to Syria by Jordan's King Abdullah II and by Mekdad's having attended the Annapolis conference. We had a thorough discussion of the important issues: the Golan Heights, Lebanon, Iran, and United States–Syrian relations. There were some informal and indirect peace talks ongoing between Syria and Israel arranged through Turkey, but Assad was very eager to have the United States involved. With peace between Israel and Syria, relationships would certainly change regarding Hamas and Hezbollah, but Syria would not endanger its important ties with Iran without overall assurance of good relations with the United States and other Western nations. The Syrians said they were working with France to resolve the long-standing stale-mate in choosing a president in Lebanon. We were impressed with the authority and mastery of details by the young president, whom I had known since he was a university student.

10

CAN HAMAS PLAY A POSITIVE ROLE?

As we prepared for our meeting with the leaders of Hamas, we were quite aware of the controversy surrounding this decision, but also of its importance. Substantive peace talks could lead to a final success only if the conclusion could have a broad base of approval among the Palestinians. There was no way to ascertain the degree of support that Hamas might have among its fellow citizens, in either Gaza or the West Bank, but the last quantifiable measure showed that 43 percent of those who had voted in January 2006 had expressed a preference for Hamas candidates. If this influential group should oppose a negotiated settlement, especially if it resorted to violence, then peace would not be possible. On the other hand, if Hamas would permit a peace process to evolve and pledge to present a neutral or positive response to an agreement, then it could be judged by Palestinians on its own merits. In the meantime, of course, a cease-fire between Hamas and Israel could reduce bloodshed, ease tensions, and enhance other positive developments.

Since it will not be possible to find peace in the Holy Land without the involvement of Hamas, I may review for the reader some (inevitably to be disputed) information about the organization. Hamas was formed in 1987, during the first intifada to oppose Israeli occupation, and its charter calls for the destruction of the State of Israel and its replacement with a Palestinian state in the Holy Land, as did the PLO charter before the Oslo Agreement negotiated by Yasir Arafat in 1993. Although the organization is based on Sunni Islamic beliefs, Hamas leaders claim that the conflict with Israel is political and not religious. They did not seek parliamentary seats when the Palestinian Authority was formed, in 1996.

When the second intifada was launched, Hamas and other militant groups resorted to suicide bombings and other acts of violence against both Israeli civilians and security forces, and from November 2000 to mid-2004 nearly four hundred Israeli citizens and soldiers were killed. At the same time, Hamas attempted to improve its standing among Palestinians by providing social services involving education, health care, and the rebuilding of homes destroyed by Israeli military forces. In August 2004, Hamas changed tactics and announced a unilateral cease-fire and pledged to forgo any attacks against Israeli civilians, but some subsequent violence was attributed to it. As early as January 2004, and again in February 2006, senior Hamas officials made public offers of a long-term truce, or *hudna*, in return for a complete withdrawal by Israel from the occupied territories and the establishment of a Palestinian state.

After their attempts to form a unity government failed in January 2006, almost all Hamas parliamentary members and proposed cabinet officers (fifty-one in all) within the West Bank were imprisoned, and about forty of them are still imprisoned. Other Hamas leaders now control Gaza or are living in exile.

We were welcomed into a private home used as headquarters by Hamas and had a long discussion with Khaled Mashaal and other leaders in the Hamas politburo, interrupted only by a supper. Unlike in other meetings I have had with fervent believers, we did not have to endure a long recitation of their grievances and a detailed presentation of their political theories. We sat facing each other in a long, narrow room, and they listened patiently while I pursued as forcefully as possible the same issues as in our Cairo meeting, including steps they might take to reduce tension, resolve some current conflicts with Israel, and enhance the prospects for progress in the peace talks under way in Jerusalem between Israeli and Palestinian leaders.

The specific things I hoped they would consider were:

(a) to accept any peace agreement negotiated between the leaders of the PLO and Israel, provided it was subsequently approved by Palestinians in a referendum or by a democratically elected government;

(b) to accept a cease-fire relating just to Gaza (they were insisting on the inclusion of the West Bank, which Israel rejected);

(c) to make progress on the prisoner exchange, with at least a letter from Corporal Shalit to his parents;

(d) to cooperate with Egypt and Israel on terms for the opening of Gaza gates;

(e) to consider a proposal for a nonpartisan professional security force in Gaza and the same arrangement for an interim Palestinian government while elections could be held; and

(f) to meet with Israel's deputy prime minister Eli Yishai.

I knew that one of the most pressing desires in Israel was the release of Gilad Shalit, an issue that we pursued aggressively. We were told that Israel had originally offered to release a thousand of the 11,600 Palestinians being held. Hamas sent a list of the first 450, but only about 70 of those were approved. We discussed an alternate way to break the stalemate: by releasing the 70, plus 41 elected Hamas legislators and 10 cabinet officers in the West Bank, and about 500 women and children, in exchange for Shalit. I also suggested that after an agreement was reached Shalit be transferred to Egypt to await the final exchange.

The Hamas leaders interrupted frequently with questions, and Mashaal gave us positive indications on some of the issues and responded cautiously to the others. We met his family, and then he, Rosalynn, Jeff, and I left about midnight while Bob Pastor, Steve Solarz, and Hrair Balian continued detailed discussions with the remaining politburo members. As Omar Suleiman had previously requested, we reported the results of our meeting to his representative so Egypt could continue discussions on the issues we had addressed.

We reassembled with the same group the following morning to summarize and clarify the points. They were to be joined over the weekend by other Hamas leaders, including those from Gaza, to consider our suggestions and provide a response before my scheduled press conference in Jerusalem after we completed the last two stops on our tour.

In the remaining two countries we had meetings with King Abdullah of Saudi Arabia, King Abdullah II of Jordan, and their key advisers. We described the purposes and some of the findings of our trip and found them to be predictably concerned about the lack of progress in peace talks between Israel and the Palestinians.

Back in Jerusalem, we received detailed responses from Hamas leaders to our ideas and then made a report to an assembly of news reporters and dignitaries at a meeting of the Israeli Council on Foreign Relations. Concerning Hamas, I said:

> I understand why Israel and other governments are reluctant to engage Hamas. They have not yet agreed to accept Israel's peaceful existence; they have not renounced violence; and they do not accept previous peace agreements. In our judgment, Hamas should accept all three points, but we do not believe peace is likely and we are certain peace is not sustainable unless a way can be found to ensure that Hamas will not disrupt the peace process.
>
> The current strategy of isolating and suppressing Hamas and persecuting the people of Gaza is not working. It only exacerbates the cycle of violence, and polls show that it may be increasing the relative popularity of Hamas throughout Palestine. Some feel that my meeting with Hamas legitimized them, but their legitimacy came when

a plurality of the Palestinian people voted for them in the 2006 elections, which I observed. Israelis know that Hamas won a majority of parliamentary seats, and a recent poll of Israeli citizens indicates strong support (64 percent) for direct Israel-Hamas talks.

To summarize the Hamas responses, either then or soon thereafter:

(a) Hamas agreed to accept any peace agreement negotiated between the leaders of the PLO and Israel provided it is subsequently approved by Palestinians in a referendum or by a democratically elected government.*

(b) Hamas agreed to a cease-fire relating just to Gaza, with final terms arranged by Omar Suleiman in Egypt. Although Israel neither denied nor confirmed any specific text, we were informed by Egypt and Hamas that the cease-fire, initiated on June 19, would continue for six months under Egyptian auspices and that crossing points would be opened initially to allow 30 percent more goods to enter Gaza and full commerce within thirteen days. Egypt would also assist in realizing the Hamas desire to

---

* There were some contrary statements made by a Hamas member on Al Jazeera television, but Mashaal confirmed all my points in a press conference in Damascus at the same time as my Israeli press conference, as we had agreed.

expand the cease-fire over time to include the West Bank. There were numerous early violations on both sides, but infractions decreased as the weeks passed. The Qassam rockets falling on Sderot ceased, Israeli military attacks in Gaza stopped, and some vital supplies of food and fuel were eventually permitted to enter Gaza. During the same time, however, Israeli incursions into the West Bank substantially escalated.

(c) After considering our prisoner proposal extensively, Mashaal informed me that their own list of 450 was a compilation of many negotiated agreements with Palestinian families and they could not violate these individual promises. They preferred that Omar Suleiman continue the discussions based on their list of names. However, we were pleased that a letter from Corporal Shalit was sent to our Ramallah office for delivery to his parents.

(d) Included in the Gaza cease-fire was a promise by Israel to permit the delivery of more supplies, and in August the Egyptians let some college students and others depart through the Rafah gate. This still left several hundred Palestinian students either without exit visas or with no assurance from Israel that they could return to their homes after studying abroad.

(e) Hamas promised to give careful consideration to a technocratic (nonpartisan) interim Palestinian government while elections could be held but insisted that the primary security force in Gaza remain under Hamas control.

(f) Hamas rejected meeting with Israel's deputy prime minister, Eli Yishai, because this might indicate an official recognition of the Israeli government.

We at The Carter Center have continued to learn what we can about the leaders of Hamas and the people under their authority. Despite the devastating economic effects of the siege of Gaza and restraints on their movement, the Hamas politburo members seemed confident, justifiably or not, that among Hamas members in the West Bank, Lebanon, and other places there would be solidarity with their positions.

In dealing with Khaled Mashaal and other Hamas leaders, I agree with other outsiders who have visited them, that a real change may be under way, especially regarding the group's willingness for Palestinians to live peacefully next to Israel. So far, few American or Israeli officials trust Hamas to do anything but seek the destruction of Israel. Knowing that Mahmoud Abbas recognizes Israel and is willing to negotiate peace, Hamas leaders assured me that they accept him as head of the PLO and president of the Palestinian Authority and therefore spokesman for all Palestinians. At the same time, they maintain that the only foundation for authority for the interim cabinet members in the West Bank comes from Jerusalem and Washington and has no legal standing since the government was established by executive order and not through free elections. They claim to be prepared for unconditional talks with Fatah, based on the agreement previously consummated at Mecca but with more attention being paid to the security forces, with advice from but not control by Egyptians or other acceptable Arabs. Both moderate and more militant Hamas leaders in Gaza and Syria claimed to us that Hamas was united in its two immediate aims: reconciliation with Fatah and a comprehensive cease-fire with Israel in both Gaza and the West Bank.

Gaza is a special place. The wall that Hamas destroyed along Egypt's border around the Rafah crossing had been a twenty-foot-high metal and concrete barrier on the Palestinian side along its entire length adjacent to Rafah city. A parallel Egyptian fence is now intact and under the watchful eyes of Egyptian border guards. There are numerous houses, shacks, and temporary installations within Gaza that are said to shelter entrances to passageways dug under the barrier. Many of the consumer products being sold in Gaza, and certainly weapons, come through these tunnels, with Hamas controlling the entry of such goods and taxing them heavily. Also, despite tight Israeli control, international funds still flow through Ramallah into Gaza—to certain citizens. When we met with Prime Minister Fayyad in April, he pointed out that full pay was going to about eighty thousand Fatah employees of his government in Gaza, although he did not permit any of them to work. This steady influx of money is a great stimulus to the isolated economy.

The primary source of Palestinian dissension regarding Gaza is the makeup of the security force. Hamas leaders have given considerable thought to a nonpartisan security force, and both sides say they "accept in principle" the idea of a unified professional force rather than party-based militias. They also acknowledge that they need help to get to that point and are willing to accept military experts and advisers from friendly Arab countries, which both parties would need to approve. However, they currently oppose a multinational peacekeeping force in Gaza.

We expressed concerns about the large number of security personnel now in Gaza—an estimated fifty-eight thousand for a population of 1.5 million. This is a ratio of one security person for every twenty-six citizens, or about eight times the ratio in New York City. Their justification for this is that the militia members have two tasks: to maintain order and to provide protection from Israeli attacks.

Although there are an increasing number of dissenters, most international leaders have demanded that Hamas meet three criteria before being given legal status: recognize Israel, accept all previously negotiated agreements, and forgo violence. The Hamas response is that (a) it will *acknowledge* Israel's right to live in peace within its pre-1967 borders, but diplomatic *recognition* can be mutual only between Israel and a sovereign Palestinian state; (b) previous agreements are not acceptable that are based on continuing Israeli occupation of Palestine (as was Oslo); and (c) it will agree to a long-term cease-fire (as much as fifty years) between Israel and an adjacent Palestinian state but not officially renounce its right to resist until Israel is no longer occupying Palestine.

Assuming that the authenticity of previous public statements and commitments to us is proven by action, there is a real prospect of Hamas participating constructively in future peace talks.

During later meetings between Pastor and Hamas leader Ismail Haniyeh, the latter provided a document containing Hamas's principles for intra-Palestinian reconciliation, which it had submitted to President Abbas. These are its positions as written, without my editing or abbreviation:

(a) Unity between the Gaza Strip and the West Bank.

(b) Unity of the Palestinian political system in the West Bank and Gaza: one authority and one government.

(c) Respect for the democratic choice and the basics of the democratic game and the commitment to its results.

(d) Government of technocrats. Hamas accepts the idea of nominating non-Hamas officials to an interim transitional government that could prepare for elections as soon as possible. Fatah and Hamas would each have a veto on the candidates.

(e) Respect for Palestinian legitimacy and what it stands for.

(f) Respect for the Palestinian basic law and commitment to it.

(g) Restructuring and rebuilding for the Palestinian security bodies on national and professional basis, and avoiding interference and quotas for parties.

(h) Commitment to the Mecca agreement (2007), Cairo agreement (2005), and the national agreement document which was approved by the Palestinian parties (2006).

(i) Commit to the right to resist as long as there is occupation.

(j) Rebuilding and activating the PLO on the basis of free elections and the participation of all Palestinian political parties.

(k) Restore the situation to the way it was before the 14th of June 2007 [when Hamas took control of Gaza] and deal with all the problems created by the Palestinian divide.

(l) Conduct presidential and parliamentary elections according to procedures and dates to be approved.

(m) Start with rebuilding of the PLO file.

We pursued the concept of nonviolent resistance with
Hamas leaders and gave them documents and video presentations on the successful experiences of Mahatma Gandhi, Mar-
tin Luther King, Jr., and others. However, they do not believe
that the Israeli occupation can be ended through such means,
because of the lack of positive response by Israel during the
relatively nonviolent early days of the first intifada.

Finally, it is interesting to note the parallel between the
Hamas of today and earlier positions of the PLO. Refusal to
accept Israel's right to exist in peace was the official PLO position before its charter was changed about five years after the
signing of the Oslo Agreement, and Hamas will have to take
similar action in accordance with any future peace agreement.
This is not an impossible prospect.

11

ASSESSMENT OF THE REGION

President Bush made a return visit to Israel in May 2008 and addressed the Israeli Knesset. There were hopes that he would repeat the dramatic statements he had made in Ramallah and Jerusalem, but he made no mention of checkpoints, settlements, Jerusalem, borders, or other key issues. The speech was a condemnation of "appeasement," as he equated any discussions with Syria, Hamas, or Iran with British prime minister Neville Chamberlain's ceding part of Czechoslovakia to Hitler's Germany in 1938. His remarks were interpreted by some to apply to my recent visits in the Middle East but mostly to Democratic presidential candidate Barack Obama's earlier announcement that under certain circumstances he would be willing to meet with foreign leaders with whom

Washington had a disagreement. Bush knew, in fact, that Israel was negotiating, through Egypt, with Hamas and that there were indirect Syria-Israel talks being sponsored by Turkey.

Feeling that key issues should not be ignored, we decided that it would be important for The Carter Center to continue to play an unofficial role in the region.

Before I describe opportunities for action or make final recommendations, it will be helpful to recapitulate the existing set of interlocking conflicts in the Middle East, including the status of relationships among Israel, Fatah, Hamas, Egypt, Syria, and Lebanon.

Geographically, the area between Lebanon, the Jordan River, Egypt, and the Mediterranean Sea is about 10,600 square miles, slightly larger than the state of Maryland. All countries that recognize Israel and the International Court of Justice accept the legal boundaries of Israel to be those existing prior to June 1967, at which point the West Bank, Gaza, the Golan Heights, and Sinai were occupied by Israeli forces. After withdrawing from Egypt's Sinai, the State of Israel comprises 77 percent of the land, with the West Bank having 22 percent and Gaza a little more than one percent. Although Israel has removed its settlers from Gaza, the official status of both Gaza and the West Bank continues to be as Israel's occupied territory, without independent sovereignty.

A succinct and somewhat harsh description was published in May 2008 by *The Economist* magazine:

> Around 5m Palestinians live in historic Palestine, under Israeli control. In the West Bank, Israeli settlements and military zones take up 40 percent of the land [see Map 1]. . . . Israel has laced the territory with walls, fences and checkpoints that box its 2.5m Palestinian residents into dozens of largely separate enclaves. Since the Islamist party, Hamas, took control of Gaza last June, its 1.5m people have been confined within the strip's 146 square miles, kept alive on a drip-feed sustenance of international aid.
>
> The 1.1m Palestinians inside Israel are far better off, though they have long suffered legal and economic discrimination. They are increasingly isolated from their brethren; Israel bars them, as its citizens, from traveling to Gaza or to most Arab countries and their cousins in the occupied territories are unable to visit them since Israel, to keep suicide bombers out, has cancelled most permits. . . . Small wonder that in a recent poll 62 percent of them expressed the fear that Israel would one day expel them. The 250,000

Palestinian residents of East Jerusalem, which Israel annexed in 1967, have Israeli residence permits. But if they move to the West Bank or travel abroad to work, they risk losing forever their right to live in the city of their birth.

The situation is different, although not better, in Gaza. On a visit to the area in June 2008, a year after Hamas assumed authority, *New York Times* reporter Ethan Bronner observed that some aspects of Islamic law were being imposed involving the charging of interest, dress codes, kissing in public, and the use of God's name in vain. Poverty was rampant, and resentment toward Israel acute. He quoted several unnamed officials as saying, "Gaza is totally under Hamas control. . . . What happened in Gaza a year ago was not really a coup. . . . The Hamas takeover was a kind of natural process. Hamas was so strong, so deeply rooted in Palestinian society through its activities in the economy, education, culture and health care, and Fatah was so weak, so corrupt, that the takeover was like wind blowing over a moth-infested structure."

Ignoring the fact that Fatah leaders were negotiating with Israel, Bronner's overall assessment was that the attitude of Hamas toward Israel was almost the same as that of Fatah and the members of the Arab League: peace and acceptance provided Israel complies with U.N. resolutions and international law. A Fatah government minister in Gaza expressed this succinct opinion: "Hamas is talking about a thirty-year truce which is no different really from what we want. Hamas is Fatah with beards."

In mid-July there was a successful prisoner exchange between Israel and Hezbollah, in which 5 Lebanese prisoners and the remains of 157 others were traded for the bodies of the 2 Israeli soldiers whose taking had precipitated the costly war in 2006. Syria's foreign minister chose this time to state that he was seeking diplomatic relations between his nation and Lebanon. Later that same month, Prime Minister Olmert announced that he would relinquish his office when the Kadima Party could choose a new leader in September, and he, Secretary Rice, and President Abbas all acknowledged that they were not likely to make any material progress on the basic peace issues.

Egyptian minister Omar Suleiman continues to play an important role in orchestrating a prisoner exchange, including the release of Corporal Shalit, and in helping to ensure compliance with the Gaza cease-fire and its extension beyond its present expiration date in December.

Unfortunately, in July 2008, Secretary Rice and Prime Minister Olmert announced that their previous commitments of a comprehensive "framework" for peace between Israel and the Palestinian Authority would not be fulfilled before the end of President Bush's term in office. Instead, there might be a statement of general principles concerning borders and some other issues. The peace process between Israel and the Palestinians reached a stalemate, and there are no leaders on either side who have the political strength and confidence of a united people to make the difficult but necessary decisions and compromises. Nobel laureates Anwar Sadat, Menachem Begin, Yitzhak Rabin, Yasir Arafat, and Shimon Peres had this influence at crucial times, as did Ariel Sharon when Israeli settlers were removed from Gaza.

Subsequently, President Abbas spoke out more strongly on behalf of Palestinian rights in opposition to settlements, the barrier wall, checkpoints, the withholding of Palestinian funds, general travel restraints, and the right of students to study abroad. In all these issues it seems that the United States has been quiescent or permissive, which further undermines Abbas's authority. His weakness is exacerbated by Israel's continuing raids in the West Bank and its separate deals with Hamas and Hezbollah.

Olmert relinquished his leadership of the Kadima Party in September, and Foreign Minister Tzipi Livni was chosen to replace him. She was unable to form a coalition government and a new election was scheduled for February 2009.

A powerful voice in favor of peace was added in late September 2008, when Prime Minister Olmert, during his last weeks in office, stated, "We have to reach an agreement with the Palestinians, the meaning of which is that in practice we will withdraw from almost all the territories, if not all the territories. We will leave a percentage of these territories in our hands, but will have to give the Palestinians a similar percentage, because without that there will be no peace. . . . Including in Jerusalem, with special solutions that I can envision on the topic of the Temple Mount and the sacred historical sites. . . . Whoever wants to hold on to all of the city's territory will have to bring 270,000 Arabs inside the fences of sovereign Israel. It won't work. A decision has to be made." He also called for Israel to be prepared to give up the Golan Heights, provided Syria will change the nature of its relationship to Hezbollah and Iran.

President Mahmoud Abbas said the Olmert remarks were a "deposit for peace," on which a comprehensive settlement could be based.

Despite Olmert's belated description of a basis for peace with Abbas, the "facts on the ground" continue to undermine the peace process based on two states. The Israeli advocacy group Peace Now reported that in the past year Israel nearly doubled its settlement construction in the occupied West Bank, in violation of its promises at Annapolis and obligations under the American-backed peace plan. For the past thirty years, there has been no doubt that in both private and public discussions, within the Holy Land and globally, the confiscation of land and building of Israeli settlements in the West Bank are recognized as one of the primary obstacles to peace. There has been a recent outpouring of condemnations by political leaders.

During a visit to Jerusalem in mid-June, Secretary Rice stated, "I am very concerned that at a time when we need to build confidence between the parties, the continued building and the settlement activity has the potential to harm the negotiations going forward." As President Bush had not mentioned settlements in his Knesset speech, the Israelis not only ignored her but announced plans to build another thirteen hundred new homes in the West Bank and projected forty thousand more during the next decade.

In quick succession, a series of other foreign leaders spoke about the negative impact of settlements. A week after the Israeli announcement, French president Nicolas Sarkozy delivered a speech to the Knesset, stating that there could not be peace in the Middle East unless Israel cedes sovereignty over parts of Jerusalem to the Palestinians and stops building settlements in the West Bank. At the same time, he reassured Israel of its security and of France's strong opposition to Iran's becoming a nuclear power.

In his first trip to Israel and the Palestinian territories as Britain's leader, Prime Minister Gordon Brown demanded that Israel cease settlement construction and promised more money to jump-start the battered Palestinian economy. Brown said, "I think the whole European Union is very clear on this matter: We want to see a freeze on settlements." The president of the European Union soon added, "This decision serves to undermine the credibility of the ongoing peace process. The building of such settlements is illegal under international law."

In an August 2008 return visit to the Middle East, Secretary Rice specifically condemned continuing Israeli construction around Hebron, the Jordan Valley, Bethlehem, Beit El, Nablus, and East Jerusalem. Israelis expressed surprise that she failed to distinguish between American opposition to the expansion of a Jewish community in the Jordan Valley and construction in the Jewish section of the Old City of Jerusalem.

Since this is such a crucial issue, it will be covered more fully in the next chapter.

Many Israelis and Americans believe that the greatest threat to Israel is the possibility of Iran's development of nuclear weapons, with missiles capable of reaching Jerusalem and Tel Aviv. Verbal threats from Iran's irresponsible leadership have exacerbated the problem. The world's leading nations seem to be unanimous in their opposition to Iran's acquiring nuclear weapons, but large numbers of centrifuges are increasingly refining nuclear materials. Iran claims they are only for peaceful production of energy, but serious doubts remain. Diplomatic deterrent efforts by European nations (supported by the United States but with little American participation) have failed, and there is constant conjecture about Israel's "taking out" Iran's nuclear facilities.

These sites are assumed to be widely dispersed and deeply buried, probably impervious to any except the most powerful weapons. Iran is far from Israel, so such a peremptory attack would require sending missiles or airplanes approximately twelve hundred miles, with flights over Jordan and either Iraq or Saudi Arabia. Even if it were successful in destroying Iran's nuclear capability, a prospect few think is likely, the results of an attack would likely be an increase in Arab support for Iran, an escalation in regional terrorism, and possibly closing of the Strait of Hormuz, through which oil from Saudi Arabia, Iraq, and other Gulf states is transported. Combining the European multilateral approach and American bilateral negotiations with Iran's more responsible leaders may be the best avenue toward a resolution of this problem.

Terrorism is a persistent threat to Israel and has created justifiable doubts in the minds of Israelis about the desire of their closest neighbors to live in peace. These threats to security have weakened moderate Israeli leaders who may be more inclined to negotiate with Palestinians in a search for common understanding. The chance for successful peace negotiations would be greatly enhanced if the threat of terrorist acts could be effectively addressed. There is little doubt that a peace agreement in the Holy Land with a contiguous and viable state for the Palestinians would remove a major cause of terrorism throughout the region.

We decided that The Carter Center would stay in contact with some of the political leaders, authors of the Geneva Accord, "elders" in Palestine and Israel, key representatives of the many peace organizations, leaders of youth groups, members of the Palestinians' Central Election Commission, Israeli and Palestinian business leaders, Fatah officials in the West Bank, Hamas leaders in Gaza and Syria, representatives of worldwide religious organizations, the various American Jewish "organizations for peace," and experts on the nonviolent resolution of conflicts. Our representatives in Ramallah continue to provide regular reports, based on their personal observations and analyses of various news media, and we added offices in Jerusalem and Gaza.

We continue to encourage a nonviolent and aggressive striving for peace, including those who in the past have resorted to violence and have been obstacles to progress. We are not naïve in believing that our words can bring about these changes, but we hope that better understanding among the antagonists might help to resolve differences when a substantive peace effort is launched.

For more than a quarter century we have worked closely with B'Tselem, Al Haq, and other courageous human rights organizations in Israel and Palestine. Remarkably effective, they monitor and report detailed information about casualties on both sides, gross violations of law, and instances of illegal abuse of innocent citizens. We help them obtain financial assistance, support their efforts to enforce the law, and join in publicizing their findings.

Carter Center staff members also monitor the status of Palestinian university students, some of them Fulbright scholars, who are deprived of visas to study abroad, and we provided funds to complete a listing of several hundred of these young people in hopes that this would assist them. Part of my Nobel Peace Prize fund assists groups of students from American universities who desire to visit the Holy Land. The most notable resulting visits have been from Emory and Brandeis, where there are high percentages of Jewish students. Their reports, now on Web sites, have been well balanced and informative about the lives of Palestinians and the possibility of improving relationships with their Israeli neighbors.

Bob Pastor and Hrair Balian have made additional visits to the region to deliver messages from me and to promote the projects outlined above, this time adding extensive visits to Lebanon. Hrair, who is in charge of our conflict resolution program, is a native of Lebanon, and he has become acquainted with key players among the political factions. The Carter Center plans to play a role in monitoring the Lebanese national elections scheduled for 2009.

12

CHALLENGES TO ISRAELIS
AND PALESTINIANS

There are some fundamental reasons why reconciliation between Israel and moderate Palestinians has been elusive. Unlike President Sadat and King Hussein, the Palestinian leaders have never learned how to gain public trust and confidence in Israel. At the same time, coalition governments in Israel have been too weak to initiate moves contrary to the concerted opposition of the smaller political factions necessary for a parliamentary majority. Under these circumstances, "security" prevails over "peace" when the two proposals are in conflict. The concept of peace has multiple connotations and can easily be projected by opponents as an uncertain route to personal and national danger. Security, however, is well understood, and the most crucial issues that can impact Israeli public opinion relate to security. A capable force (Palestinian and international) that could maintain order in Palestine and protect Israelis from violence would go a long way in convincing the Israeli public to make needed compromises for peace. It is almost inevitable that the United States play a leadership role in such an effort to convince the Israeli public that such commitments will be honored.

Lacking military or political strength of their own, Palestinians have had to depend on the international community to represent their interests. They have seen specific commitments of the United Nations, the International Quartet, the Arab League, and a series of negotiators from the United States made, perhaps trusted, and then abandoned. Their dream and all the peace proposals have been predicated on the basic concept of an Israeli and a Palestinian community living side by side in peace. At least in recent years, this "two-state" concept has been the prevailing vision of Israel. This basic premise is now being threatened.

After the announcements that seemed to spell the end of the post-Annapolis peace talks, our Carter Center team in Ramallah began reporting a shift in the attitude of Palestinian leaders with whom they were meeting:

> Failure of the negotiations following Annapolis may well mark an end to the two-state solution for Israel and Palestine. Without progress on the peace talks, a profound change in opinion is

taking place. Palestinians, both in the country and in the Diaspora, are beginning to look at those Palestinians who are Israeli citizens—albeit with restricted rights—and compare their condition to living under occupation. The conclusion seems to be that even second class Israeli citizenship is preferable to unending occupation, or in other terms, the future may lie in one state. If Palestinians were given the choice between having a non-sovereign state without Jerusalem and being part of a one-state solution, they will choose the latter.

This may be an unwarranted conclusion, but it is certainly a growing point of view. Whether he was making a serious threat or not, in mid-August the top Palestinian negotiator, Ahmed Qurei (Abu Ala), announced in Ramallah, "If Israel continues to reject our propositions regarding the borders [of a future Palestinian state], we might demand Israeli citizenship." He went on to list the issues covered by U.N. resolutions, the Geneva Accord, the Quartet's Roadmap, and the Arab peace offer. Referring to the proliferation of Israeli settlements within the West Bank, Fatah leader Qaddurah Fares, a strong supporter of a two-state solution, asked, "Where will the Palestinian state rise up? The Israeli nation is inside us already" (see Map 1). In a private meeting with our Carter

Center staff, one of the most influential Palestinian spokespersons, Hanan Ashrawi, said that Israel is "heading toward a de facto one-state solution where Palestinian communities would become totally disconnected from each other."

Sari Nusseibeh, the highly respected president of the Arab Al-Quds University in Jerusalem, has also been a strong supporter of a two-state solution, but in July 2008 he said, "I know that people assume . . . that it will always be possible to arrive at two states, but I don't think so." Absent an agreement on Palestinian statehood, he added, "We will have to prepare ourselves for the next stage." The next stage within a single state would be a struggle before world opinion for equal political rights for millions of Palestinian voters similar to what took place in South Africa. The two-state goal is still being given lip service, but a *New York Times* analysis in September 2008 confirmed a strong change in preference among moderate Palestinians toward a single state as the only way to resolve the prolonged deadlock in peace negotiations. This might obviate the long-term prospect of a Jewish state, the historic Zionist goal.

Within one nation Palestinians would soon have a majority of citizens—and voters—leading to either the end of a Jewish state or the legal deprivation of voting rights among second-class Palestinians. With equal Palestinian status under the law, an analysis of settlement areas would reveal the extent of the taking and control of privately owned Palestinian territory and the disparity in treatment between Israeli settlers and native Palestinians. It may also force Israel to assume financial responsibility for what is left of Palestine (and to provide for Gaza).

This is a prospect that many Israelis have feared for many years and an ancient subject of debate within the Jewish community. The crucial decision can be made only by the people of Israel, and the outcome of all future peace efforts will depend on the answer.

In 1999, former prime minister and now minister of defense Ehud Barak told *The Jerusalem Post*, "Every attempt to keep hold of this area as one political entity leads, necessarily, to either a non-democratic or a non-Jewish state. Because if the Palestinians vote, then it is a bi-national state, and if they don't vote it is an apartheid state that might then become another Belfast or Bosnia."*

In an interview with *Yediot Aharonot* in December 2003, then vice prime minister Olmert said, "Above all hovers the cloud of demographics. It will come down on us not in the end of days, but in just another few years. We are approaching a point where more and more Palestinians will say: 'There is no place for two states between the Jordan and the sea. All we want is the right to vote.' The day they get it we will lose everything."

---

* Both places were then in civil conflict.

More recently, in November 2007, Prime Minister Olmert said to *Haaretz* that if the two-state solution collapsed, Israel would "face a South African–style struggle for equal voting rights, and as soon as that happens, the state of Israel is finished." He warned that "the Jewish organizations, which were our power base in America, will be the first to come out against us because they will say they cannot support a state that does not support democracy and equal voting rights for all its residents."

Within Israel there has been a long-standing fundamental struggle between two powerful political forces: those who wish to preserve the purity of Judaism and others who wish to increase the population of a "Jewish state" throughout the Holy Land. The Orthodox, whose political support is crucial to the formation of a coalition government in the Knesset, control the Rabbinical Court system, with authority over conversions, marriages, and divorces. They impose tight restrictions on who can become a Jew. To them, one must be born of a Jewish mother into the faith or be able to prove an ability and willingness to abide by the very strict laws and commandments that govern an observant Jew's daily life. Ariel Sharon expressed the dilemma of many prominent secular Jews in clear and vivid terms: "If I had to convert, I would not pass."

Many religious Jews welcome converts and encourage settlement in the Holy Land, which helps to delay the time when there will be a majority of non-Jews living between the Jordan

River and the Mediterranean Sea. Some extremists would favor depriving Arab Israelis of equal voting rights or expulsion so they will not constitute a majority. So far, the increase in Arab population through higher birthrates has been substantially matched by an influx of Diaspora Jews. The dwindling number of immigrants from America and other Western nations (there may now be a net exodus) has been counterbalanced by about a million newcomers from the former Soviet Union, many of whom have retained their former language and customs and tend to vote as a bloc. They now make up about one-sixth of the Jewish population. A number of these families have doubtful credentials to prove their Jewish ancestry.

The struggle between the Rabbinical Court and the more secular government ministries is not likely to be resolved at any time in the near future, but it is interesting to note that the influence of ultra-Orthodox families is growing. This group, known as the *haredi*, receive a high level of government funding for their special schools and social programs and do not serve in the military. They have a much higher birthrate than do other Jews and are projected to double their portion of Israel's population to about 20 percent within the next two decades.*

---

* The most recent population estimates are that there are 5,552,000 Jews and 5,385,000 Arabs in the Holy Land, plus about 318,000 other non-Jews. A higher percentage of the Arabs are younger and not yet of voting age. The 1,477,000 Arabs in Israel make up about one-fifth of the total population and now hold twelve seats in the Knesset, but they have never accumulated the influence of other

Some fervent Zionists have promoted the expansion of settlements on Palestinian land. Although opposed by a majority of Israelis, the drive for settlements in Palestine has prevailed until now because of general unwillingness to face the unpleasant prospect of removing those settlers who are most militant.

Palestinians, Israelis, and other observers recognize that during the past sixteen years, U.S. political leaders have acquiesced in Israel's massive settlement building in East Jerusalem and the West Bank. Intended to establish permanent "facts on the ground," the result has been to diminish (or eliminate) the prospect of a sovereign, contiguous, and viable Palestinian state with the West Bank linked to Gaza and its capital in East Jerusalem.

A precursor of withholding Palestinian voting rights is already evident. As reported in earlier chapters, stringent steps have been taken in every election to prevent Palestinian residents of East Jerusalem from participating in choosing their own leaders. At the end of April 2008, members of the Palestinian Central Election Commission had gone to almost eight hundred schools throughout the West Bank to update the voter rolls by registering seventeen-year-olds, but officials who sought to carry out this procedure in East Jerusalem were

---

voting blocs. They are now becoming more isolated from fellow Israelis and increasingly identified with their Palestinian relatives.

arrested and their official registration materials were confiscated by the Israelis.

Two of Israel's basic military and political goals have been (a) to prevent any threat to its people or state and to ensure Israel's ability to defend itself, and (b) to secure universal international and regional acceptance as a member of the community of nations. Israel's military force is modern, highly trained, and superior to the combined forces of all its potential adversaries, especially since Egypt was removed thirty years ago as a potential combatant. In addition, Israel has a formidable nuclear arsenal. Its small size, however, makes it vulnerable to a potential attack from any source. Israel has diplomatic relations with all except thirty-four nations, but two of its neighbors, Lebanon and Syria, consider themselves to be at war with Israel.

For Palestinians, there is a special relationship with Israel and divisions within their own ranks. Despite elections in 1996 and 2006 to form a unified Palestinian Authority to govern the occupied territories, there is now de facto Hamas control over Gaza and an elected president with an interim government, not approved by parliament, in the West Bank serving under overall Israeli military and political control. Efforts by Saudi Arabia and others to reforge a unity government between the two Palestinian factions have been frustrated by animosity between the two major parties and opposition from Israel, the United States, and most of the international community because of Hamas's failure to meet the requirements of the International Quartet.

A tenuous Gaza cease-fire between Israel and Hamas has been negotiated under Egyptian auspices, but there is no similar agreement applicable to the West Bank. Within the same mediating framework, there are continuing efforts to consummate an exchange of Israeli corporal Shalit for a large number of Palestinian prisoners held by Israel.

In most Arab nations and among the leaders of Fatah and Hamas, we found a desire for reconciliation of the two Palestinian factions and a conviction that without this accommodation there could be no substantive progress toward peace between Israel and its closest neighbors. There are two main goals that must be realized, as outlined by Palestinian leaders on both sides: an adequate security force in the West Bank and Gaza to maintain order and prevent violence, and a caretaker government in Palestine that can organize elections for president and parliamentary seats.

A final status agreement between Israel and the Palestinians will require a security force in the occupied territories that can guarantee the security of Israel and Palestine and the people in both countries. Palestinians are unlikely to accept any final agreement that does not include the withdrawal of the Israel Defense Forces from their territory, and Israel is unlikely to accept any arrangement that would permit an attack on Israel from a Palestinian state. It is almost certain that both requirements can be met only by an international peacekeeping force that is backed strongly by the United States, in both its inception and its fulfillment. With Palestinian unity, this force can meet this need in both Gaza and the West Bank. Such an international security force would require a clear mandate and the ability to prevent any acts of violence against Israel and Israeli citizens, and Israel would also have to guarantee that it would not intervene in Palestine. Ideally, this mandate would be fully approved also by the Arab nations, NATO, and the United Nations.

The other step will be formation of a transition government of nonpartisan leaders, acceptable to both Fatah and Hamas, under which elections can take place to form a permanent and united Palestinian government. Hamas will have to accommodate the basic conditions of the International Quartet before its candidates can participate in government.

According to respected human rights organizations, there has been a recent escalation of violence among the Palestinians, under both Fatah and Hamas. Detention without trial, abuse of prisoners, harassment of critics, and pressure on nongovernmental organizations are increasingly prevalent in the West Bank and Gaza. The Carter Center adopted a special project to work with human rights organizations to reduce these abuses, realizing that the best solution is reconciliation between the Palestinian factions.

An impending political crisis is that Mahmoud Abbas's term as president arguably expires in January 2009 and elections are not scheduled until 2010. The constitution prescribes that his successor be the speaker of the Legislative Council, who is one of the elected Hamas legislators and not permitted to serve. If Abbas decides to stay in office, he could probably do so and have the same authority as Fayyad and other nonelected officials who are now governing in the West Bank. If he should decide to step down, then it is possible that the International Quartet could make some binding, semi-legal decisions about a successor.

Perhaps the most important overarching decision for the Palestinians is whether to seek equal citizenship within a single nation instead of continuing their frustrated struggle for separate statehood. The Israelis will have to provide the ultimate response.

Tragically, there are few normal contacts in the fields of politics, trade and commerce, tourism, education, arts, or culture between Israelis and Palestinians or even among the "friendly" nations pledged to peace (Jordan, Egypt, and Israel). Nor do these nations join forces with the United States to heal the open wounds that alienate Israel from the Palestinians, Lebanon, and Syria. It seems that none of the four really wants such a working coalition.

The other Arab nations, led by Saudi Arabia, are kept at arm's length by the United States and Israel but have repeatedly offered to be of assistance in forging a regional peace agreement. An end to strife and uncertainty would be beneficial to all of them. Their offer of peace and diplomatic recognition to Israel is predicated on compliance with key U.N. resolutions, especially 242 and 194.

The key differences between Israel and the Palestinians concern how to comply with applicable U.N. resolutions concerning borders, Jerusalem, refugee issues, and security.

Again, American leadership and involvement have been lacking but are key to an agreement. From the United States' side an ancillary potential benefit is the possibility of Syria's increased cooperation in achieving our goals in Iraq, the promotion of peace in Lebanon, and reduction of terrorism in the region. American cooperation will also be required in resolving other Israel-Syria issues involving water rights, the environment, and trade.

13

AN AGENDA FOR PEACE

Despite all the discouraging news, there are some positive developments in the region that we should remember. Arab leaders have reconfirmed their 2002 offer of peace with Israel: diplomatic recognition and normal economic relations, based on Israel's compliance with basic U.N. resolutions. Any differences or modifications can be resolved, as they have declared, through "direct and serious negotiations on all tracks." Secretary of State Condoleezza Rice has recommended the 2002 offer of the twenty-two Arab nations as a foundation for peace, and Israeli leaders have characterized the Arab offer as "a starting point for talks." Palestinian president Mahmoud Abbas stated, "If this initiative is destroyed, I do not believe that a better chance for peace will present itself in the near future." It is interesting to note that this proposal was also approved in 2003 by all fifty-seven Islamic nations (thirty-five of them non-Arabic), including an affirmative vote from Iran's moderate president, Mohammad Khatami.

Syria: Syria is a key factor in any overall regional peace, but President Bush has refused to support Syria's peace talks with Israel on the Golan Heights or even to engage Syria on a bilateral basis. Indirect Israeli-Syrian discussions, sponsored by Turkey, are evidence that the two protagonists are willing to seek a resolution of their differences. If Israel and Syria were at peace, then Syrian influence might also become a positive factor in Lebanon.

A resolution of the Golan Heights issue is necessary for regional peace, but Israelis are understandably opposed to any deal that would make Israel's border with Syria vulnerable. The principles of an agreement based on Israel's withdrawal have been known since I was consulting in the region more than twenty years ago with Hafez al-Assad and Yitzhak Shamir. The general terms are: (a) a multinational peace force and a buffer zone on the Golan to prevent any cross-border violence; (b) Israel to have riparian rights along the east side of the Sea of Galilee to permit north-south travel; (c) excellent surveillance and early warning; and (d) peace with Syria equivalent to that with Egypt and Jordan. As a result of negotiations between 1994 and 2000, the two parties agreed on most outstanding issues and filed an unsigned affirmation with the U.S. State Department. According to Turkish intermediaries, the United States withdrew its opposition to the Syrian-Israeli negotiations in June 2008, but was still not supportive. In fact, President Assad announced early in September that the talks with Israel were being postponed until after Israel and the United States have new leaders.

There is now a possible resolution of the difficult Israeli demand for a corridor along the east side of the Sea of Galilee. The level of the lake has fallen because of heavy irrigation, and an area of the shoreline is exposed that is not part of the original Syrian territory.

Lebanon: The Lebanese government's inherent instability and the aftermath of the Israeli-Lebanese war of July 2006 have made it impossible for this troubled nation to be a positive factor in regional peace, but relative calm has prevailed since a new president, Michel Suleiman, was elected in May 2008. With Syria's political influence reduced, there is hope that elections in 2009 will bring a long-overdue era of domestic tranquillity—and a chance of peace with Israel if the Palestinian issue can be resolved. Another positive factor has been the July 2008 agreement between Israel and Hezbollah for the release of the last Lebanese prisoners in Israel and the exchange of human remains from both sides.

One of the most hotly contested parcels of land in the Middle East is Shebaa Farms, comprising only eight square miles, which Israel continues to occupy. It is through this part of the border that all Israeli invasions into Lebanon have been launched. The farms are strategically located near Syria's Golan Heights and control access roads to Israeli positions on nearby Mount Hermon. Shebaa Farms cannot be addressed independently from other issues, including the fate of the Israeli-Syrian talks. The basic argument is whether the place belongs to Syria or Lebanon, with Israel claiming it is Syria's and therefore part of its occupation of the Golan Heights. If the land is Lebanon's, which Syria has recently acknowledged to be the case, then Israel is obligated to withdraw without further delay. The United Nations has the responsibility of demarcating Lebanon's borders with Israel and Syria, so the dispute may be resolved peacefully when this survey is completed if Israel is assured that Shebaa Farms will not be used by Hezbollah for aggression.

In Lebanon, the Doha peace agreement, the end of massive opposition protests, the election of a consensus president, and the establishment of relations with Syria have brought the country back from the brink of renewed civil war. Plans are under way for an election in 2009 that could yield the formation of a government of national unity, living in peace with Israel.

Egypt: The leaders of Egypt are fairly satisfied with its status in the region, enjoying benefits from the peace treaty with Israel and American financial assistance. It is now playing a limited but useful role as a mediator in the intra-Palestinian disputes, between Hamas and Israel in probing for a prisoner exchange, managing the southern border with Gaza, and nurturing the Israel-Hamas cease-fire that has been in place in and around Gaza since June 2008. The Egyptians are very careful not to assume responsibility for the administration of Gaza and not to permit any substantial movement of Palestinians, especially Hamas supporters, into Egypt. Its own government uses every means to prevent the development of any real domestic political opposition, and the U.S. government is acquiescent regarding these restraints on civil liberties.

Palestine: On several public occasions and to me personally, Hamas leaders have offered to accept any peace agreement negotiated between Israel and PLO leaders if it is approved by Palestinians in a referendum or by a freely elected government. Although Hamas prefers a more comprehensive cease-fire with Israel that includes the West Bank, the agreement limited to Gaza has been helpful in reducing violence by stopping the rocket attacks on Israel and the retaliatory attacks on Gaza.

There is strong support for a united Palestinian government, as indicated by a September 2008 poll in the West Bank and Gaza. It showed that 87 percent of the Palestinians want the current caretaker government to resign in exchange for a unity government—a requisite first step toward comprehensive peace talks. Absent a unified Palestinian government, there is a respected moderate leader, Mahmoud Abbas, who is recognized by a strong majority of Palestinians as authorized to represent their cause in substantive peace negotiations with

Israel. Marwan Barghouti, if released from prison by Israel, may be more acceptable to both major Palestinian parties and more effective in peace talks with Israel. There are some feeble attempts to close the rift between Fatah and Hamas, but mutual animosity and opposition from the United States and Israel now preclude any prospect for success.

Israel: The premise of real peace and security in exchange for Palestinian territory has long been acceptable to a substantial majority of Israelis but not to a minority of the more conservative leaders, who are unfortunately supported by most of the vocal American Jewish leadership.

A generic decision that must be made is whether the actual goal in the Holy Land is a two-state solution, as is presently the official commitment of Israel, the United States, the Palestinian Authority, and the international community. If so, the potentially disastrous moves toward one state must be terminated. These include occupation of the West Bank and the Jordan River valley, with hopeless prospects for a viable, contiguous, and sovereign Palestinian state. This leaves a separate, suffering, and antagonistic Gaza.

I am familiar with the harsh rhetoric and extreme acts of violence in the Middle East that have been perpetrated against innocent civilians and understand the fear among many Israelis of the threats that still exist against their safety and even their existence as a nation. Unfortunately, excessive levels of violence between Israelis and Palestinians have continued, as one side launches attacks and the other responds. Predictably, both claim to be just retaliating.

There is clear proof that a cessation of violence is not a hopeless prospect when a vision of peace exists. There were few significant acts of violence during these all-too-rare times, such as when the Camp David Accords and Israeli-Egyptian peace treaties were being consummated, during the Madrid conference and on to Oslo, and later during the Palestinian elections of 1996, 2005, and 2006.

I know from personal experience that the influence of our government is limited, but there is no prospect for regional harmony and stability unless the United States plays a leadership role in strongly espousing proposals that include the essential components of pertinent United Nations resolutions, the Roadmap of the International Quartet, the Oslo Agreement, the peace offer of the Arab nations endorsed by other Muslim states, the Camp David Accords, and the Geneva Accord. At one time or another, both Israel and the Palestinians have accepted these same basic terms. Obviously, close attention must be paid to the special concerns of both sides, but there is an excellent prospect of these being harmonized through good-faith negotiations.

To be permanently honored, as the peace treaties between Israel and both Egypt and Jordan are, an agreement must prove to be beneficial to both sides, with any requisite sacrifices or compromises clearly outweighed by advantages. The crucial factors are peace *and* security, which if established in the Holy Land would ease tensions and the threat of violence in a much wider geographical region. Even the prospect of a costly showdown with Iran would be lessened if both the United States and Israel could have stable and friendly diplomatic and trade relations with now-antagonistic factions in Palestine and with Lebanon, Syria, and all other Arab nations. Facing a united front in the region against any Iranian nuclear ambitions could be a deciding factor in convincing leaders in Tehran to abandon their potentially suicidal plans.

In addition to supporting settlement of the Golan Heights dispute, the United States can shape a comprehensive peace effort between Israel and the Palestinians, but this can happen only if the president is willing to address this complex and sensitive subject courageously and early in his first term. The most difficult step is to spell out and endorse the difficult compromises that must be made by both Israelis and Palestinians and then use persuasion and enticements to reach these reasonable goals with the full backing of other members of the International Quartet and the Arab nations. With details to be resolved by the two sides but with active assistance from

America, the basic framework to be proclaimed by the president would include:

• A demilitarized Palestinian state, with the Israel Defense Forces replaced by a mutually acceptable international security force effective enough to prevent violence against either side, to guard against militarization, and to allow freedom of peaceful movement;

• Mutually acceptable modifications, with land swaps, to the 1967 border to permit a number of Israelis to retain their homes in and around Jerusalem, and withdrawal of all other settlers from the West Bank;

• A sharing of Jerusalem, which would be the capital of both states, with special rights of Jews and Muslims within their holy sites and joint governance of other areas of the Old City;

• The right of Palestinians to return to the West Bank and Gaza and compensation for those with proven claims in Israel;

• A separate but forceful commitment to reconciliation of the Palestinians and unity between Gaza and the West Bank, with requirements that the two states, Palestine and Israel, recognize the mutual right to live side by side in peace;

• A specific time limit should be set for the consummation of these goals, or at least an assessment of progress made and difficulties remaining, perhaps in September 2009.

As I wrote in 1985, "The blood of Abraham, God's father of the chosen, still flows in the veins of Arab, Jew, and Christian, and too much of it has been spilled in grasping for the inheritance of the revered patriarch in the Middle East. The spilled blood in the Holy Land still cries out to God—an anguished cry for peace." It is time to replace anguish with joy and celebration.

U.N. RESOLUTION 242, 1967

UNITED NATIONS SECURITY COUNCIL
RESOLUTION 242, NOVEMBER 22, 1967

The Security Council,

Expressing its continuing concern with the grave situation in the Middle East,

Emphasizing the inadmissibility of the acquisition of territory by war and the need to work for a just and lasting peace in which every State in the area can live in security,

Emphasizing further that all Member States in their acceptance of the Charter of the United Nations have undertaken a commitment to act in accordance with Article 2 of the Charter,

1. Affirms that the fulfillment of Charter principles requires the establishment of a just and lasting peace in the

Middle East which should include the application of both the following principles:

(i) Withdrawal of Israeli armed forces from territories occupied in the recent conflict;

(ii) Termination of all claims or states of belligerency and respect for and acknowledgment of the sovereignty, territorial integrity and political independence of every State in the area and their right to live in peace within secure and recognized boundaries free from threats or acts of force;

2. Affirms further the necessity

(a) For guaranteeing freedom of navigation through international ways in the area;

(b) For achieving a just settlement of the refugee problem;

(c) For guaranteeing the territorial inviolability and political independence of every State in the area, through measures including the establishment of demilitarized zones;

3. Requests the Secretary-General to designate a Special Representative to proceed to the Middle East to establish and maintain contacts with the States concerned in order to promote agreement and assist efforts to achieve a peaceful and accepted settlement in accordance with the provisions and principles of this resolution.

4. Requests the Secretary-General to report to the Security Council on the progress of the efforts of the Special Representative as soon as possible.

Appendix 2

———— •◆•————

CAMP DAVID ACCORDS, 1978

A FRAMEWORK FOR PEACE IN THE MIDDLE EAST AGREED AT CAMP DAVID

Agreed To at Camp David, September 17, 1978

Muhammad Anwar al-Sadat, President of the Arab Republic of Egypt, and Menachem Begin, Prime Minister of Israel, met with Jimmy Carter, President of the United States of America, at Camp David from September 5 to September 17, 1978, and have agreed on the following framework for peace in the Middle East. They invite other parties to the Arab-Israeli conflict to adhere to it.

PREAMBLE

The search for peace in the Middle East must be guided by the following:

—The agreed basis for a peaceful settlement of the conflict between Israel and its neighbors is United Nations Security Council Resolution 242, in all its parts.*

—After four wars during thirty years, despite intensive human efforts, the Middle East, which is the cradle of civilization and the birthplace of three great religions, does not yet enjoy the blessings of peace. The people of the Middle East yearn for peace so that the vast human and natural resources of the region can be turned to the pursuits of peace and so that this area can become a model for coexistence and cooperation among nations.

—The historic initiative of President Sadat in visiting Jerusalem and the reception accorded to him by the Parliament, government and people of Israel, and the reciprocal visit of Prime Minister Begin to Ismailia, the peace proposals made by both leaders, as well as the warm reception of these missions by the people of both countries, have created an unprecedented opportunity for peace which must not be lost if this generation and future generations are to be spared the tragedies of war.

---

* The texts of Resolutions 242 and 338 are annexed to this document.

—The provisions of the Charter of the United Nations and the other accepted norms of international law and legitimacy now provide accepted standards for the conduct of relations among all states.

—To achieve a relationship of peace, in the spirit of Article 2 of the United Nations Charter, future negotiations between Israel and any neighbor prepared to negotiate peace and security with it, are necessary for the purpose of carrying out all the provisions and principles of Resolutions 242 and 338.

—Peace requires respect for the sovereignty, territorial integrity and political independence of every state in the area and their right to live in peace within secure and recognized boundaries free from threats or acts of force. Progress toward that goal can accelerate movement toward a new era of reconciliation in the Middle East marked by cooperation in promoting economic development, in maintaining stability, and in assuring security.

—Security is enhanced by a relationship of peace and by cooperation between nations which enjoy normal relations. In addition, under the terms of peace treaties, the parties can, on the basis of reciprocity, agree to special security arrangements such as demilitarized zones, limited armaments areas, early warning stations, the presence of international forces, liaison, agreed measures for monitoring, and other arrangements that they agree are useful.

Framework

Taking these factors into account, the parties are determined to reach a just, comprehensive, and durable settlement of the Middle East conflict through the conclusion of peace treaties based on Security Council Resolutions 242 and 338 in all their parts. Their purpose is to achieve peace and good neighborly relations. They recognize that, for peace to endure, it must involve all those who have been most deeply affected by the conflict. They therefore agree that this framework as appropriate is intended by them to constitute a basis for peace not only between Egypt and Israel, but also between Israel and each of its other neighbors which is prepared to negotiate peace with Israel on this basis. With that objective in mind, they have agreed to proceed as follows:

A. West Bank and Gaza

1. Egypt, Israel, Jordan and the representatives of the Palestinian people should participate in negotiations on the resolution of the Palestinian problem in all its aspects. To achieve that objective, negotiations relating to the West Bank and Gaza should proceed in three stages:

(a) Egypt and Israel agree that, in order to ensure a peaceful and orderly transfer of authority, and taking into account the security concerns of all the parties, there should be transitional arrangements for the West Bank and

Gaza for a period not exceeding five years. In order to provide full autonomy to the inhabitants, under these arrangements the Israeli military government and its civilian administration will be withdrawn as soon as a self-governing authority has been freely elected by the inhabitants of these areas to replace the existing military government. To negotiate the details of a transitional arrangement, the Government of Jordan will be invited to join the negotiations on the basis of this framework. These new arrangements should give due consideration both to the principle of self-government by the inhabitants of these territories and to the legitimate security concerns of the parties involved.

(b) Egypt, Israel, and Jordan will agree on the modalities for establishing the elected self-governing authority in the West Bank and Gaza. The delegations of Egypt and Jordan may include Palestinians from the West Bank and Gaza or other Palestinians as mutually agreed. The parties will negotiate an agreement which will define the powers and responsibilities of the self-governing authority to be exercised in the West Bank and Gaza. A withdrawal of Israeli armed forces will take place and there will be a redeployment of the remaining Israeli forces into specified security locations. The agreement will also include arrangements for assuring internal and external security and public order. A strong local police force will be established, which may include Jordanian

citizens. In addition, Israeli and Jordanian forces will participate in joint patrols and in the manning of control posts to
assure the security of the borders.

      (c) When the self-governing authority (admin-
istrative council) in the West Bank and Gaza is established
and inaugurated, the transitional period of five years will begin. As soon as possible, but not later than the third year after
the beginning of the transitional period, negotiations will take
place to determine the final status of the West Bank and Gaza
and its relationship with its neighbors, and to conclude a peace
treaty between Israel and Jordan by the end of the transitional
period. These negotiations will be conducted among Egypt,
Israel, Jordan, and the elected representatives of the inhabitants of the West Bank and Gaza. Two separate but related
committees will be convened, one committee, consisting of
representatives of the four parties which will negotiate and
agree on the final status of the West Bank and Gaza, and its
relationships with its neighbors, and the second committee,
consisting of representatives of Israel and representatives of
Jordan to be joined by the elected representatives of the inhabitants of the West Bank and Gaza, to negotiate the peace
treaty between Israel and Jordan, taking into account the
agreement reached on the final status of the West Bank and
Gaza. The negotiations shall be based on all the provisions
and principles of U.N. Security Council Resolution 242. The

negotiations will resolve, among other matters, the location of the boundaries and the nature of the security arrangements. The solution from the negotiations must also recognize the legitimate rights of the Palestinian people and their just requirements. In this way, the Palestinians will participate in the determination of their own future through:

1) The negotiations among Egypt, Israel, Jordan and the representatives of the inhabitants of the West Bank and Gaza to agree on the final status of the West Bank and Gaza and other outstanding issues by the end of the transitional period.

2) Submitting their agreement to a vote by the elected representatives of the inhabitants of the West Bank and Gaza.

3) Providing for the elected representatives of the inhabitants of the West Bank and Gaza to decide how they shall govern themselves consistent with the provisions of their agreement.

4) Participating as stated above in the work of the committee negotiating the peace treaty between Israel and Jordan.

2. All necessary measures will be taken and provisions made to assure the security of Israel and its neighbors during the transitional period and beyond. To assist in providing such security, a strong local police force will be consti-

tuted by the self-governing authority. It will be composed of inhabitants of the West Bank and Gaza. The police will maintain continuing liaison on internal security matters with the designated Israeli, Jordanian, and Egyptian officers.

3. During the transitional period, representatives of Egypt, Israel, Jordan, and the self-governing authority will constitute a continuing committee to decide by agreement on the modalities of admission of persons displaced from the West Bank and Gaza in 1967, together with necessary measures to prevent disruption and disorder. Other matters of common concern may also be dealt with by this committee.

4. Egypt and Israel will work with each other and with other interested parties to establish agreed procedures for a prompt, just, and permanent implementation of the resolution of the refugee problem.

B. Egypt-Israel

1. Egypt and Israel undertake not to resort to the threat or the use of force to settle disputes. Any disputes shall be settled by peaceful means in accordance with the provisions of Article 33 of the Charter of the United Nations.

2. In order to achieve peace between them, the parties agree to negotiate in good faith with a goal of concluding within three months from the signing of this Framework a peace treaty between them, while inviting the other parties to the conflict to proceed simultaneously to negotiate and conclude similar peace treaties with a view to achieving a

comprehensive peace in the area. The Framework for the Conclusion of a Peace Treaty between Egypt and Israel will govern the peace negotiations between them. The parties will agree on the modalities and the timetable for the implementation of their obligations under the treaty.

C. Associated Principles

1. Egypt and Israel state that the principles and provisions described below should apply to peace treaties between Israel and each of its neighbors—Egypt, Jordan, Syria, and Lebanon.

2. Signatories shall establish among themselves relationships normal to states at peace with one another. To this end, they should undertake to abide by all the provisions of the Charter of the United Nations. Steps to be taken in this respect include:

(a) full recognition;

(b) abolishing economic boycotts;

(c) guaranteeing that under their jurisdiction the citizens of the other parties shall enjoy the protection of the due process of law.

3. Signatories should explore possibilities for economic development in the context of final peace treaties, with the objective of contributing to the atmosphere of peace, cooperation, and friendship which is their common goal.

4. Claims Commissions may be established for the mutual settlement of all financial claims.

5. The United States shall be invited to participate in the talks on matters related to the modalities of the implementation of the agreements and working out the timetable for the carrying out of the obligations of the parties.

6. The United Nations Security Council shall be requested to endorse the peace treaties and ensure that their provisions shall not be violated. The permanent members of the Security Council shall be requested to underwrite the peace treaties and ensure respect for their provisions. They shall also be requested to conform their policies and actions with the undertakings contained in this Framework.

For the Government of the Arab Republic of Egypt:
        A. Sadat

For the Government of Israel:
        M. Begin

Witnessed by:
        Jimmy Carter
        President of the United States of America

Appendix 3

ARAB PEACE PROPOSAL, 2002

THE ARAB LEAGUE "PEACE PLAN,"
MARCH 28, 2002

The Council of the League of Arab States at the Summit
Level, at its 14th Ordinary Session;

Reaffirming the resolution taken in June 1996 at the Cairo
Extraordinary Arab Summit that a just and comprehensive
peace in the Middle East is the strategic option of the Arab
Countries, to be achieved in accordance with International
Legality, and which would require a comparable commitment
on the part of the Israeli Government.

Having listened to the statement made by His Royal Highness Prince Abdullah Bin Abdullaziz, the Crown Prince of the

Kingdom of Saudi Arabia in which his Highness presented his Initiative, calling for full Israeli withdrawal from all the Arab territories occupied since June 1967, in implementation of Security Council Resolutions 242 and 338, reaffirmed by the Madrid Conference of 1991 and the land for peace principle, and Israel's acceptance of an independent Palestinian State, with East Jerusalem as its capital, in return for the establishment of normal relations in the context of a comprehensive peace with Israel.

Emanating from the conviction of the Arab countries that a military solution to the conflict will not achieve peace or provide security for the parties, the council:

1. Requests Israel to reconsider its policies and declare that a just peace is its strategic option as well.

2. Further calls upon Israel to affirm:

a. Full Israeli withdrawal from all the territories occupied since 1967, including the Syrian Golan Heights to the lines of June 4, 1967, as well as the remaining occupied Lebanese territories in the south of Lebanon.

b. Achievement of a just solution to the Palestinian Refugee problem to be agreed upon in accordance with UN General Assembly Resolution 194.

c. The acceptance of the establishment of a Sovereign Independent Palestinian State on the Palestinian territories occupied since the 4th of June 1967 in the West Bank and Gaza Strip, with East Jerusalem as its capital.

3. Consequently, the Arab Countries affirm the following:

a. Consider the Arab-Israeli conflict ended, and enter into a peace agreement with Israel, and provide security for all the states of the region.

b. Establish normal relations with Israel in the context of this comprehensive peace.

4. Assures the rejection of all forms of Palestinian patriation which conflict with the special circumstances of the Arab host country.

5. Calls upon the government of Israel and all Israelis to accept this initiative in order to safeguard the prospects for peace and stop the further shedding of blood, enabling the Arab countries and Israel to live in peace and good neighbourliness and provide future generations with security, stability and prosperity.

6. Invites the international community and all countries and organisations to support this initiative.

7. Requests the chairman of the summit to form a special committee composed of some of its concerned member states and the secretary-general of the League of Arab States to pursue the necessary contacts to gain support for this initiative at all levels, particularly from the United Nations, the Security Council, the United States of America, the Russian Federation, the Muslim states and the European Union.

———•◆•———

KEY POINTS OF THE INTERNATIONAL QUARTET'S ROADMAP FOR PEACE, APRIL 30, 2003

A settlement, negotiated between the parties, will result in the emergence of an independent, democratic, and viable Palestinian state living side by side in peace and security with Israel and its other neighbors. The settlement will resolve the Israel-Palestinian conflict, and end the occupation that began in 1967, based on the foundations of the Madrid Conference, the principle of land for peace, United Nations Security Council Resolutions 242, 338, and 1397, agreements previously reached by the parties, and the initiative of Saudi Crown Prince Abdullah—endorsed by the Beirut Arab League Summit—calling for acceptance of Israel as a neighbor living in peace and security, in the context of a comprehensive settlement. This initiative is a vital element of international efforts to promote a comprehensive peace on all tracks, including the Syrian-Israeli and Lebanese-Israeli tracks.

PHASE I

In Phase I, the Palestinians immediately undertake an unconditional cessation of violence according to the steps outlined below; such action should be accompanied by supportive measures undertaken by Israel. Palestinians and Israelis resume security cooperation. Palestinians undertake comprehensive political reform in preparation for statehood, including drafting a Palestinian constitution, and free, fair, and open elections upon the basis of those measures. Israel takes all necessary steps to help normalize Palestinian life. Israel withdraws from Palestinian areas occupied from September 28, 2000, and the two sides restore the status quo that existed at that time, as security performance and cooperation progress. Israel also freezes all settlement activity.

At the outset of Phase I:

- Palestinian leadership issues unequivocal statement reiterating Israel's right to exist in peace and security and calling for an immediate and unconditional cease-fire to end armed activity and all acts of violence against Israelis anywhere. All official Palestinian institutions end incitement against Israel.

• Israeli leadership issues unequivocal statement affirming its commitments to the two-state vision of an independent, viable, sovereign Palestinian state living in peace and security alongside Israel, as expressed by President Bush, and calling for an immediate end to violence against Palestinians everywhere. All official Israeli institutions end incitement against Palestinians.

• Palestinians declare an unequivocal end to violence and terrorism and undertake visible efforts on the ground to arrest, disrupt, and restrain individuals and groups conducting and planning violent attacks on Israelis anywhere.

• Rebuilt and refocused Palestinian Authority security apparatus begins sustained, targeted, and effective operations aimed at confronting all those engaged in terror and at dismantlement of terrorist capabilities and infrastructure. This includes commencing confiscation of illegal weapons and consolidation of security authority, free of association with terror and corruption.

• Government of Israel [GOI] takes no actions undermining trust, including deportations, attacks on civilians; confiscation and/or demolition of Palestinian homes and property, as a punitive measure or to facilitate Israeli construction; destruction of Palestinian institutions and infrastructure; and other measures specified in the Tenet Work Plan.

• All Palestinian security organizations are consolidated into three services reporting to an empowered interior minister.

- Restructured/retained Palestinian security forces and IDF [Israel Defense Forces] counterparts progressively resume security cooperation and other undertakings in implementation of the Tenet Work Plan, including regular senior-level meetings, with the participation of U.S. security officials.

- Arab states cut off public and private funding and all other forms of support for groups supporting and engaging in violence and terror.

- All donors providing budgetary support for the Palestinians channel these funds through the Palestinian Ministry of Finance's Single Treasury Account.

- As comprehensive security performance moves forward, IDF withdraws progressively from areas occupied since September 28, 2000, and the two sides restore the status quo that existed prior to September 28, 2000. Palestinian security forces redeploy to areas vacated by IDF.

- As rapidly as possible, constitutional committee circulates draft Palestinian constitution, based on strong parliamentary democracy and cabinet with empowered prime minister, for public comment/debate. Constitutional committee proposes draft document for submission after elections for approval by appropriate Palestinian institutions.

- Appointment of interim prime minister or cabinet with empowered executive authority/decision-making body.

- GOI fully facilitates travel of Palestinian officials for Palestine Legislative Council [PLC] and cabinet sessions, internationally supervised security retraining, electoral and other reform activity, and other supportive measures related to the reform efforts.

- Establishment of independent Palestinian election commission. PLC reviews and revises elections law.

- Palestinian performance on judicial, administrative, and economic benchmarks, as established by the International Task Force on Palestinian Reform.

- As early as possible, and based upon the above measures and in the context of open debate and transparent candidate selection/electoral campaign based on a free, multiparty process, Palestinians hold free, open, and fair elections.

- GOI facilitates Task Force election assistance, registration of voters, movement of candidates and voting officials. Support for NGOs involved in the election process.

- GOI reopens Palestinian Chamber of Commerce and other closed Palestinian institutions in East Jerusalem based on a commitment that these institutions operate strictly in accordance with prior agreements between the parties.

- Israel takes measures to improve the humanitarian situation. Israel and Palestinians implement in full all recommendations to improve humanitarian conditions, lifting curfews, and easing restrictions on movement of persons and goods, and allowing full, safe, and unfettered access of international and humanitarian personnel.

• GOI and Palestinian Authority continue revenue clearance process and transfer of funds, including arrears, in accordance with agreed, transparent monitoring mechanism.

• GOI immediately dismantles settlement outposts erected since March 2001.

• Consistent with the Mitchell Report, GOI freezes all settlement activity (including natural growth of settlements).

PHASE II

In the second phase, efforts are focused on the option of creating an independent Palestinian state with provisional borders and attributes of sovereignty, based on the new constitution, as a way station to a permanent status settlement. As has been noted, this goal can be achieved when the Palestinian people have a leadership acting decisively against terror, willing and able to build a practicing democracy based on tolerance and liberty. With such a leadership, reformed civil institutions and security structures, the Palestinians will have the active support of the Quartet and the broader international community in establishing an independent, viable state.

Progress into Phase II will be based upon the consensus judgment of the Quartet of whether conditions are appropriate to proceed, taking into account performance of both parties. Furthering and sustaining efforts to normalize Palestinian lives and build Palestinian institutions, Phase II starts after Palestinian elections and ends with possible creation of an independent Palestinian state with provisional borders in 2003. Its primary goals are continued comprehensive security performance and effective security cooperation, continued normalization of Palestinian life and institution-building, further building on and sustaining of the goals outlined in Phase I, ratification of a democratic Palestinian constitution, formal establishment of office of Prime Minister, consolidation of political reform, and the creation of a Palestinian state with provisional borders.

- Arab states restore pre-intifada links to Israel (trade offices, etc.).
- Revival of multilateral engagement on issues including regional water resources, environment, economic development, refugees, and arms control.
- New constitution for democratic, independent Palestinian state is finalized and approved by appropriate Palestinian institutions. Further elections, if required, should follow approval of the new constitution.
- Empowered reform cabinet with office of Prime Minister formally established, consistent with draft constitution.

• Creation of an independent Palestinian state with provisional borders through a process of Israeli-Palestinian engagement, launched by the international conference. As part of this process, implementation of prior agreements, to enhance maximum territorial contiguity including further action on settlements in conjunction with establishment of a Palestinian state with provisional borders.

• Quartet members promote international recognition of Palestinian state, including possible UN membership.

PHASE III

• Continued comprehensive, effective progress on the reform agenda laid out by the Task Force in preparation for final status agreement.

• Continued sustained and effective security performance, and sustained, effective security cooperation on the basis laid out in Phase I. International efforts to facilitate reform and stabilize Palestinian institutions and the Palestinian economy, in preparation for final status agreement.

• Parties reach final and comprehensive permanent status agreement that ends the Israel-Palestinian conflict in 2005, through a settlement negotiated between the parties based on United Nations Security Council Resolutions 242, 338, and 1397, that ends the occupation that began in 1967, and includes an agreed, just, fair, and realistic solution to the refugee issue, and a negotiated resolution on the status of

Jerusalem that takes into account the political and religious concerns of both sides, and protects the religious interests of Jews, Christians, and Muslims worldwide, and fulfills the vision of two states, Israel and sovereign, independent, democratic and viable Palestine, living side-by-side in peace and security.

• Arab state acceptance of full normal relations with Israel and security for all the states of the region in the context of a comprehensive Arab-Israeli peace. Also see http://www.state.gov/r/pa/prs/ps/2003/20062.htm.

ISRAEL'S RESPONSE TO THE ROADMAP FOR PEACE, MAY 25, 2003

1. Both at the commencement of and during the process, and as a condition to its continuance, calm will be maintained. The Palestinians will dismantle the existing security organizations and implement security reforms during the course of which new organizations will be formed and act to combat terror, violence and incitement (incitement must cease immediately and the Palestinian Authority must educate for peace). These organizations will engage in genuine prevention of terror and violence through arrests, interrogations, prevention and the enforcement of the legal groundwork for investigations, prosecution and punishment. In the first phase of the plan and as a condition for progress to the second phase, the Palestinians will complete the dismantling of terrorist organizations (Hamas, Islamic Jihad, the Popular Front, the

Democratic Front Al-Aqsa Brigades and other apparatuses) and their infrastructure, collection of all illegal weapons and their transfer to a third party for the sake of being removed from the area and destroyed, cessation of weapons smuggling and weapons production inside the Palestinian Authority, activation of the full prevention apparatus and cessation of incitement. There will be no progress to the second phase without the fulfillment of all above-mentioned conditions relating to the war against terror. The security plans to be implemented are the Tenet and Zinni plans. (As in the other mutual frameworks, the Roadmap will not state that Israel must cease violence and incitement against the Palestinians.)

2. Full performance will be a condition for progress between phases and for progress within phases. The first condition for progress will be the complete cessation of terror, violence and incitement. Progress between phases will come only following the full implementation of the preceding phase. Attention will be paid not to timelines, but to performance benchmarks. (Timelines will serve only as reference points.)

3. The emergence of a new and different leadership in the Palestinian Authority within the framework of governmental reform. The formation of a new leadership constitutes a condition for progress to the second phase of the plan. In this framework, elections will be conducted for the Palestinian Legislative Council following coordination with Israel.

4. The Monitoring mechanism will be under American management. The chief verification activity will concentrate upon the creation of another Palestinian entity and progress in the civil reform process within the Palestinian Authority. Verification will be performed exclusively on a professional basis and per issue (economic, legal, financial) without the existence of a combined or unified mechanism. Substantive decisions will remain in the hands of both parties.

5. The character of the provisional Palestinian state will be determined through negotiations between the Palestinian Authority and Israel. The provisional state will have provisional borders and certain aspects of sovereignty, be fully demilitarized with no military forces, but only with police and internal security forces of limited scope and armaments, be without the authority to undertake defense alliances or military cooperation, and Israeli control over the entry and exit of all persons and cargo, as well as of its air space and electromagnetic spectrum.

6. In connection to both the introductory statements and the final settlement, declared references must be made to Israel's right to exist as a Jewish state and to the waiver of any right of return for Palestinian refugees to the State of Israel.

7. End of the process will lead to the end of all claims and not only the end of the conflict.

8. The future settlement will be reached through agree-

ment and direct negotiations between the two parties, in accordance with the vision outlined by President Bush in his 24 June address.

9. There will be no involvement with issues pertaining to the final settlement. Among issues not to be discussed: settlement in Judea, Samaria and Gaza (excluding a settlement freeze and illegal outposts), the status of the Palestinian Authority and its institutions in Jerusalem, and all other matters whose substance relates to the final settlement.

10. The removal of references other than 242 and 338 (1397, the Saudi Initiative and the Arab Initiative adopted in Beirut). A settlement based upon the Roadmap will be an autonomous settlement that derives its validity therefrom. The only possible reference should be to Resolutions 242 and 338, and then only as an outline for the conduct of future negotiations on a permanent settlement.

11. Promotion of the reform process in the Palestinian Authority: a transitional Palestinian constitution will be composed, a Palestinian legal infrastructure will be constructed and cooperation with Israel in this field will be renewed. In the economic sphere: international efforts to rehabilitate the Palestinian economy will continue. In the financial sphere: the American-Israeli-Palestinian agreement will be implemented in full as a condition for the continued transfer of tax revenues.

12. The deployment of IDF forces along the September

2000 lines will be subject to the stipulation of Article 4 (absolute quiet) and will be carried out in keeping with changes to be required by the nature of the new circumstances and needs created thereby. Emphasis will be placed on the division of responsibilities and civilian authority as in September 2000, and not on the position of forces on the ground at that time.

13. Subject to security conditions, Israel will work to restore Palestinian life to normal: promote the economic situation, cultivation of commercial connections, encouragement and assistance for the activities of recognized humanitarian agencies. No reference will be made to the Bertini Report as a binding source document within the framework of the humanitarian issue.

14. Arab states will assist the process through the condemnation of terrorist activity. No link will be established between the Palestinian track and other tracks (Syrian-Lebanese).

ACKNOWLEDGMENTS

———◆———

The search for peace in the Middle East is a challenging task, and it is very difficult to understand the complex inter-relationships among the people who contend with one another in the region. I am indebted to the staff of The Carter Center, who remain deeply immersed in the region, who have monitored all Palestinian elections, and who provide me with current information and advice on changing circumstances. David Carroll directs the Democracy Program. The Director of the Conflict Resolution Program is Hrair Balian, a native of Lebanon, who has special understanding of the reasons for the ongoing conflicts and shares the personal yearning for peace that exists among his own kinsmen and among the Israelis and their other Arab neighbors. Karin Ryan is in charge of the Human Rights Program, the conscience of The Carter Center.

I am especially indebted to Dr. Robert Pastor. He has

made the advance trips to prepare for our visits to the region, has participated personally in our wide range of discussions with key leaders and private citizens, and has provided useful suggestions to help ensure that this book is both balanced and accurate. He was responsible for inviting Steve Solarz to accompany us on our April 2008 trip. Steve served as a senior member of the House Foreign Affairs Committee for eighteen years and was one of the leading proponents of Israeli peace and security in Congress. He was already familiar with most of the key issues and leaders in the region and proved to be a great asset as we probed for better knowledge and understanding. Several of the participants in the Camp David peace negotiations of 1978 provided valuable information and advice, including Zbigniew Brzezinski, William Quandt, Sam Lewis, and my wife, Rosalynn.

As always, Steve Hochman checked the accuracy of the text, and Lauren Gay helped to ensure that my communication with my good publisher, Simon & Schuster, was prompt and reliable. As with many of my other books, Alice Mayhew provided invaluable editorial assistance. I should add that, in all cases, I made the final decisions about the substance and wording of the text.

INDEX

ABOUT THE AUTHOR

JIMMY CARTER was born in Plains, Georgia, and served as thirty-ninth President of the United States. He and his wife, Rosalynn, founded The Carter Center, a nonprofit organization that prevents and resolves conflicts, enhances freedom and democracy, and improves health around the world. He is the author of numerous books, including *An Hour Before Daylight*, called "An American classic," and the #1 New York Times bestseller *Our Endangered Values*. He was awarded the Nobel Peace Prize in 2002.